Just before the start of the 2002 Wales versus Scotland match in Cardiff, the stadium announcer asked people to stand and acknowledge Bill McLaren's great contribution to rugby. The whole ground rose, leaving McLaren choking back the tears. Then came a voice in his ear: 'Cue, Bill . . .'

Critical Acclaim for Bill McLaren

www.booksattransworld.co.uk

MY AUTOBIOGRAPHY

Bill McLaren

with Peter Bills

BANTAM BOOKS

LONDON • TORONTO • SYDNEY • AUCKLAND • JOHANNESBURG

MY AUTOBIOGRAPHY
A BANTAM BOOK : 0 553 81558 X

Originally published in Great Britain by Bantam Press,
a division of Transworld Publishers

PRINTING HISTORY
Bantam Press edition published 2004
Bantam edition published 2005

1 3 5 7 9 10 8 6 4 2

Set in 12/16.75pt Sabon by
Falcon Oast Graphic Art Ltd.

Bantam Books are published by Transworld Publishers,
61–63 Uxbridge Road, London W5 5SA,
a division of The Random House Group Ltd,
in Australia by Random House Australia (Pty) Ltd,
20 Alfred Street, Milsons Point, Sydney, NSW 2061, Australia,
in New Zealand by Random House New Zealand Ltd,
18 Poland Road, Glenfield, Auckland 10, New Zealand
and in South Africa by Random House (Pty) Ltd, Isle of Houghton,
Corner Boundary Road & Carse O'Gowrie, Houghton 2198, South Africa.

Printed and bound in Great Britain by
Cox & Wyman Ltd, Reading, Berkshire

Papers used by Transworld Publishers are natural, recyclable
products made from wood grown in sustainable forests. The
manufacturing processes conform to the environmental
regulations of the country of origin

To Bette

Bill McLaren has been a legend within the business of sports broadcasting for an extraordinary fifty years and during that time, rugby fans throughout the world will have been brought up learning from Bill's knowledgeable comments, or seduced by his melodious tones to watch for a bit longer. His unique contribution to the commentator's art has been applauded by both his peers and listeners alike the world over.

But Bill McLaren has done a great deal more for the sport he loves than simply commentate on it. Under his shrewd tutelage, untold numbers of aspiring young rugby players have learned the game in the Scottish Borders. Through his many years as a teacher, he has inculcated not merely the technical requirements of the game to young people but perhaps, just as importantly, the social responsibilities of young rugby men in terms of expected standards of decency and behaviour. The game could not have had a finer tutor or one more suited to represent it and pass on its timeless virtues than Bill McLaren.

I have enjoyed meeting Bill and his wife Bette on many occasions and it has always been a pleasure to see them. It is no wonder to me that Bill has been honoured by so many people for his myriad contributions to the world of rugby football. He has passed on his love for the game and all it represents to everyone he has met or spoken with. Both Scotland and the game itself could not have had a better ambassador and as Patron of Scottish Rugby I am grateful for this opportunity to write the foreword to the autobiography of his whole life. I know you will enjoy reading the book which is a fitting testament to Bill's love of life and rugby.

Anne

CONTENTS

CHAPTER 1

THE DAY IT ENDED

I'D SOMETIMES HAD NIGHTMARES ABOUT THIS MOMENT. There I would be, comfortably settled into my seat somewhere high up in the stand at some rugby ground, and I'd be all ready for the big day and my commentary. I had done all the preparatory work, filled out my 'prompt chart' with every bit of relevant information I could possibly want to cover any eventuality. The microphone, one of those funny old metal ones with a bar that goes across your mouth, would be in my hand. I would be ready and waiting for the familiar 'Cue Bill'. But when I started talking behind the live pictures being beamed from the stadium, no sound came out. Then the frantic voice of the producer in my earpiece: 'Bill, we're live – Go.' I tried again, but the same thing happened: I'd be talking but no one could hear a word I was saying.

I woke up each time I tried to turn up the volume

in my voice, so I never found out what happened next and whether I kept my job. Thankfully, nothing like that ever occurred in real life. But at the end of my career something else happened that pulled the rug from beneath my feet and almost undermined all my dedicated preparation for commentary, all the hours of effort I always put into it.

That day came at Cardiff's Millennium Stadium on 6 April 2002. It was the day of my final broadcast for BBC Television, and it is one I shall never forget.

It was fifty years since my first rugby match as a commentator. Travelling down to Wales on the Thursday evening prior to the last weekend of that season's Six Nations Championship, I turned over in my mind some of the events of those fifty years. Half a century of being invited to go and watch rugby matches all over Scotland, the British Isles, Europe and even as far afield as South Africa, Australia and New Zealand. All at someone else's expense, and for a very acceptable salary. I have had to pinch myself at some stage of every one of those fifty years to make sure that I wasn't imagining it, fearing that someone might shake me and bring me down to earth, where I would sadly discover it had all been a dream.

Being paid to do what you love is a wonderful way of life, I can tell you. Frankly – and of course I never told the BBC this – I would probably have done it all for nothing if they had merely offered me the chance and said, 'Of course, we can't afford to pay you as well.' Because this was the job I had always coveted, always fantasised about doing. From my earliest days, I always wanted to be a commentator, initially, back then, for radio. It was like inviting a Scottish schoolboy to play rugby for Scotland and adding that, by the way, he'd be very well paid for it, too. How fortunate are some folk?

I had been in awe of the Welsh national ground the first time I went to the old Cardiff Arms Park to cover a rugby international. I had heard so much about people like Vivian Jenkins and Wilf Wooller, great Welsh players of the 1930s, not to mention the wonderful deeds enacted on that famous turf. It was never the loveliest stadium in the Five Nations countries, but for raw emotion it was unique, in my experience.

In those days, I used to go down to Cardiff on the Thursday evening after work and stay at the Angel Hotel. Apart from being a most friendly place, it was right across the street from the Arms Park so I could pop over on Friday mornings and watch the Welsh squad train on the Cardiff Athletic ground that backs on to the main stadium. Cardiff still has a special atmosphere for me. It is the singing, I think, that is the distinctive thing with the Welsh people. When 65,000 of them start singing, especially 'Land of my Fathers', it is very emotional and gives the team a huge fillip. And when their national anthem is played, I defy anyone to remain unmoved. Someone once said to me in the early days that playing at Cardiff was worth a five-point start to the Welsh team, and I could understand that. For visiting sides, it must have seemed formidable. It can't have been easy to keep your thoughts in the right order in the face of such a vocal challenge.

I had the clear impression in my mind that in many respects the Welsh were special. They were different. There had always been a buzz of excitement on the rare occasions when my club Hawick played a Welsh club. One year, back in the 1930s when I was nine or ten years old, I was sitting in the stand alongside my father when a strong Newport team came up to Mansfield Park from south Wales. They included what I thought was a huge full-back, W. A. Everson, a man so large he seemed to defy the conventional mould for a full-back at that time. I remember him kicking a goal from the halfway line with the toe of his boot, and that really was something out of the ordinary then. Those old leather rugby balls were like dead weights when they became wet. How players ever hoofed them high enough to get them over the crossbar I'll never know.

There was a real aura about that Newport side that gave us a sense that they were to be revered. And everything they did that day, the way they looked and the manner in which they played, justified that aura. They met a Hawick team that included my hero, Willie Welsh. At one stage, Welsh had to leave the field briefly for attention to an eye injury. It seemed that all Hawick held its breath before the great man returned, for we badly needed him. Hawick just managed to scrape a 6–3 win that day, and the seed of respect for Welsh rugby was sown deep in my mind.

It was special, too, when Wales travelled to Scotland for an international. I can still see the old Murrayfield ground clearly in my mind's eye, with that vast stretch of open terracing on the far side of the ground, opposite the main stand, just one enormous splurge of scarlet. The fact that their supporters came up to Scotland in their thousands left a big impression on me of the Welshman's fierce hunger for rugby football. Even today, the Welsh arrive in droves for the Scotland–Wales fixture.

Many of them stay in the Scottish Borders that weekend; indeed, our region is all but taken over for the duration. It is a delight to have them, because in its love of the game, my home territory is very like south Wales.

The great Gareth Edwards once told me that when he was in Scotland one year, early in the week of the Welsh international, he had gone down to Kelso, in the Borders, to do a spot of salmon-fishing. There he was, out in his waders in the middle of the river, when a local chap poked his head over the nearby bridge and said, 'Good God, what are you doing, Gareth?'

Gareth couldn't resist it. 'Hello. I'm just signing a few autographs,' he replied, and the chap apparently walked off, scratching his head.

I had always felt that in Wales rugby was bred in the bone, that their people loved the game with a passion perhaps unmatched anywhere else. Getting to know some of their most outstanding players of the eras that followed only enhanced my respect for the Welsh game.

The more I thought about it, as I made the familiar journey to Cardiff for my final broadcast, the more I felt I had seen the best days of rugby football. There had been lean years, certainly, such as those of the early 1960s, when rugby in the British Isles was stuck in a rut and I feared the game was dying on its feet. In one match between Scotland and Wales at Murrayfield that I covered during that period there were 111 line-outs. One hundred and eleven. I know because when I went home and watched the tape, I counted every single one of them. I nearly fell asleep doing so, mind you.

Miraculously, after plummeting to such depths (and remember, the British Lions lost the Test series on three successive tours to the southern hemisphere in the 1960s alone), daylight began to emerge at the end of the dark alleyway into which the sport had stumbled. By the opening of the 1970s, a strong sun was shining down on our game once again, initially in the form of some wonderfully talented young Welsh boys with names such as J.P.R. Williams, Gerald Davies, John Dawes, Barry John and a certain Gareth Edwards.

Wales were to dominate the seventies, through those fine threequarters and also with some skilful forwards, men of great power and immense ability such as Mervyn Davies, Delme Thomas, John Taylor, Derek Quinnell and the legendary Pontypool front row of Charlie Faulkner, Bobby Windsor and Graham Price. But that strong undercurrent of brilliant Welshmen did more than just make Wales a powerful rugby team. It underpinned successive British Lions touring sides to New Zealand in 1971 and South Africa in 1974. So much so that those two tours became the most successful in Lions history, a worthy testimony to a quite magnificent era.

Of course, other countries contributed too. None more so than Ireland, with the likes of Willie John McBride and Mike Gibson, and England with David Duckham and Fran Cotton. Then there was my beloved Scotland, with star players like the flying Scot Andy Irvine and big Gordon Brown, the renowned late 'Broon of Troon' who, together with his fellow Lions forwards, rumbled across the big, parched fields of South Africa in 1974 like horses on the hoof. All played their part in making so many of the Five Nations Championship matches of the 1970s truly special. And, as Max Boyce, that fine Welsh comedian, likes to say, 'I was there.' In fact, I'd have walked all the way from my home in Hawick to Wales to be there. The standard of play between 1969 and 1979 was as good as anything I have ever seen during my long career in the game.

Then there were the times when the mighty touring teams from the southern hemisphere rugby countries of South Africa, Australia and New Zealand came to

Britain. As part of my 'homework' for the match days I would always attend the visitors' training sessions on Friday mornings, spending long hours watching intently, studying individual players' features and trying to memorise each in conjunction with face and name so that I would be able to identify them instantly in my commentary. Homework was a crucial element.

I worked intensely throughout, attending to my own needs, and most teams did not mind me being there at all. But then there were the French. Now, my French language skills and their Scottish ones rarely met harmoniously, with the result that my requests for access to their training sessions were, initially at least, greeted with deep suspicion. 'Eet ees a spy, no?' they were probably thinking to themselves as I prowled up and down the touchline, studying a sweaty, squashed Gallic face accessorised by horrible, chewed-up cauliflower ears.

It probably won't surprise you to hear that my favourite rugby country, after Scotland, obviously, would have been Wales. Not only had the Welsh people provided me with over half a lifetime of great memories of superb rugby football, but I always enjoyed meeting and talking to them. I had a good rapport with them right from the first time I went to

Cardiff, and they always made me feel most welcome. To me, they remain what their national team once was: really special. They are warm, friendly, down-to-earth, bereft of fuss and usually to be seen with smiles on their faces, happy and laughing. They seem to have a naturally cheerful disposition. And, of course, they have that deep love and respect for rugby and its traditions, for which I admire them immensely. Unlike some, they can acknowledge and applaud fine examples of skill on the field from the opposition. I like that, too.

I think one of the reasons I got on well with the Welsh people was that I studied the laws of the game, and tactics, too, so I was able to embellish my commentary with little bits here and there that I had picked up in my formative years, either playing for or watching Hawick, and they grew increasingly responsive to my efforts. Mind you, you needed to be on the alert for the Welsh wit that came flying around your head like bits of shrapnel. It could be a touch cutting, as they say, and you had to be ready with a suitable response.

After so many years of what I regarded as a close affinity with Wales, I felt it was perhaps appropriate that I was to end my days as a television commentator at the principality's famous ground. The memories I had of great matches played there, of marvellous characters and brave men, were the essence of rugby football. I loved the atmosphere of Cardiff on match days. Welsh rugby headquarters has always been sited right in the heart of the city. On international days, there is a natural buzz around the whole of Cardiff which you don't really find at any other inter-national rugby venue I can think of. Grounds such as Twickenham and the Stade de France in Paris are a train ride out of their home cities, while even Murrayfield and Lansdowne Road are a walk away from the centres of Edinburgh and Dublin respectively. But in Cardiff, great bus and train loads of supporters are decanted straight into the city centre, which creates a fabulous mood. Everywhere you go, the talk is of the match.

When the French come to Cardiff on the morning of the game, you can hear the first strains from the musicians of the famous Dax band coming down the street long before you see them. Then you'll notice little pockets of Frenchmen carrying banners with the names of some of the traditional rugby towns in the south – Agen, Béziers, Biarritz, Clermont-Ferrand, Narbonne, Perpignan and Toulouse. Those wonderful Basque bands play lively music wherever they go.

Inside the stadium, there will always be one French supporter releasing a live cockerel on to the field of play. It will run around in the kind of bemusement and confusion you might expect of a farmyard bird being roared or laughed at by anything up to 60,000 or 70,000 people.

There have been so many great matches at Cardiff down the years. I can remember watching dear old Alex Hastie, the former Melrose scrum-half, on a filthy day in Cardiff in the 1960s when it rained and rained. The old Arms Park was a swamp, and the Scottish forwards kept putting the ball back to him. For long spells of that match, Hastie was what we call in Scotland a 'drookit rat' – soaked to the skin. He had mud all over his face and in his hair, and his jersey and shorts were coated in the stuff. Yet he gave the bravest performance I had ever seen from a Scotland scrum-half in Cardiff. He fell on the ball to halt the Welsh charges, picked it up and got clobbered, and just kept tidying up the mess his forwards had left him. Shovelling the ball back anyhow in those conditions was a liability, but Hastie just got on with it. He was still there at the end, the mud dripping off his eyebrows, his ears, everywhere. He looked such a sight. But I thought he should have been awarded the Victoria Cross for that display. He was kicked and stood on, trampled and walked all over by the Welsh pack, and he must have almost drowned once or twice when he ended up face-down in the mud. But in spite of his efforts, I don't think Scotland won, from what I can remember. In my view, modern-day forwards are much more aware of what their half-backs need in the way of quality ball. They know that if they fail in their job of securing and supplying good possession, then their scrum-half and fly-half are going to be the first ones to feel the effect.

The Welsh national team might no longer be as pre-eminent as they were in that golden era, but loyalty to the game in the principality remains strong. How else would you explain the fanatical support Wales continue to receive whenever they play? Why else, when the Millennium Stadium was being built, did crowds of 60,000 or more regularly make the long journey all the way up the M4 to London to see them play at their temporary home at Wembley? Spectators often had to return home disappointed, but the day their team beat England there in 1999 must have made it all worthwhile.

Truth to tell, 2002 had not been a vintage season for the International Championship by any stretch of the imagination. There were worrying signs that a championship within a championship was emerging, with England and France putting themselves in a class of their own. Of course, these two great rugby nations have always had much larger pools of talent on which to draw for their sides. We used to joke up in Scotland that England could choose three teams to win the Championship if anyone ever told them how to go about the selection process. For years, they didn't seem able to get their show on the road in terms of planning, proper preparation and consistent selection. But by the time professionalism came along in 1995, England had at last started to translate their latent power into success on the field.

France had always had power and potential. In the late 1960s and 1970s, when Wales had been the only show in town, it was the French who went with them, participating in some classic encounters in Cardiff and Paris. No one else could match the pair of them in that era of high quality and class on anything other than a very occasional basis.

But this season had been different. Leaving aside the performances of England and France, you had to admit there had been some woeful displays by the other four countries in the now-expanded tournament of six nations. Wales, for example, had gone to Dublin in February for their first game and been completely humiliated, 54–10 – six tries to one. I shuddered for my many Welsh friends; I knew what they would be feeling, and it was not pleasant. Yet a fortnight later, when Wales confronted the mighty French on their home territory in Cardiff, and all the press boys had doubtless packed their pocket calculators to keep up with the anticipated cricket score, they very nearly achieved the upset of the season. The match ended with Wales, 37–33 behind, pounding the French line and having two lunges for the try-line stopped by inches. That was what I had always loved about this great championship: the element of the unexpected. That one side, in the depths of despair after a heavy defeat, could somehow rally and, just fourteen days later, almost pull off a feat no one had envisaged.

Wales didn't quite manage it that day but they had gone on to beat Italy 44–20 before suffering another big defeat, a 50–10 reverse at the hands of the big boys in the shape of the English at Twickenham.

Scotland, meanwhile, had lurched equally alarmingly through the season. An opening-day 29–3 loss to England at Murrayfield was every bit as conclusive as the result suggests. They won 29–12 in Italy, but there then followed defeats by Ireland, 43–22 in Dublin – a match in which that marvellous, highly talented centre Brian O'Driscoll scored a hat-trick of tries for his country – and France, 22–10 at Murrayfield.

For the final weekend of the Championship, England were in Rome to play Italy on the Sunday, and were inevitably heavy favourites against the young, exciting rugby nation. But, having lost to France in Paris in a titanic clash, they had given France the chance to win the title and the Grand Slam if they could beat Ireland in Paris on the Sunday.

So, should I choose Paris or Cardiff as the venue for my final television commentary from a Six Nations Championship game? That earlier remark I made about fortunate folk came once more to mind. But it was always going to be Cardiff for me. The BBC were covering the game live in Cardiff, whereas they would be taking a picture feed of the other match from French TV in Paris. Besides, in my heart I wanted to go to Cardiff. I knew it would be a special feeling sitting up there in that magnificent new stadium they had created in time for the 1999 World Cup, which Wales had hosted.

I like the Millennium Stadium. It seems to me that the designers got it exactly right in terms of the pitch of the huge stands that quickly began to dominate the Cardiff skyline when building began in the mid-1990s. At some of the modern international rugby grounds, the stands rise backwards well away from the field, and the spectators are an awful long way away from the action. If you happen to be sitting at the very top of one of the towering stands at Twickenham or the Stade de France in Paris, you have as good a view, so people tell me, of nearby Richmond or the Eiffel Tower as you do of the match taking place far below you. The old Twickenham stadium was a great example of one where the crowd was right on top of the field, and it brought the spectators much closer to the players.

Who could forget, for example, that day in 1970 when the immortal Tony O'Reilly played his last game for Ireland, at Twickenham – seven years after what he had thought had been his international farewell. In the interim O'Reilly had been working for the giant American food company H.J. Heinz Ltd, spending much of his time sitting in board meetings and being ferried around in one of the company's chauffeured limousines, so he was, shall we say, hardly in the best condition of his long and distinguished career. So when the ball was kicked to Ireland's wing on a grim, wet winter's afternoon in London, it stopped dead in the mud right in front of him. There was no time to pick it up and start running – the England forwards were closing fast on their quarry. O'Reilly did what a man has to do in those circumstances. He went down on the loose ball on the ground and took the knocks and blows from the onrushing English feet.

When at last the great man's torment had been ended by the referee's whistle, a dazed O'Reilly sat up on the sodden Twickenham turf and tried to wipe off half the mud of London. During the lull in proceedings, an Irish voice in the crowd called out: 'And yer can kick his f****** chauffeur, too!' That one brought most of the players to their knees with laughter, as well as all the fans in that part of the stand. It was this intimacy that made those old grounds so unique. Having grown up in the days when the adults pushed us wee youngsters down the steps to the front by the fence at Murrayfield so that we would have a better view, I loved them for it.

In Cardiff they seem to have managed to create a smart new stadium without losing the intimacy of the place. The stands rise almost perpendicularly from the pitch side, and there is not too much of a gap between the turf and the first rows of spectators, which gives you the sense of being much more packed in, in the nicest sense.

I took my designated seat in our lofty eyrie on that early spring day and surveyed the scene below me. There was the familiar sea of red, the thousands of Welsh supporters who, through thick and thin, support their team loyally. The grass was a vivid green, fresh and inviting, as it seems to look everywhere these days for a big international match. I chuckled quietly to myself at the memory of all those Arms Park mud-heaps on which I had watched international games played down the years. Sometimes you could hardly recognise which team had the ball once the game got underway and the mud began to fly. Some matches seemed more like a version of the Eton wall game than a game of rugby. I remember Gareth Edwards once breaking downfield, kicking ahead and winning the race to the touchdown, and sliding on over the dead-ball line into the liquid red shale behind the pitch. When he got up and ran back to the halfway line with his colleagues, he looked like some creation from the sculptor's table brought to life. I'd never seen anything like it.

Having settled into my commentary position, I opened up my faithful old briefcase. Here I carried the working accoutrements of a television commentator, the tools of my trade. I was like teacher out for a day with his pupils: just about every eventuality was catered for. Spare pencils, rubbers, sheets of paper, a stopwatch, an ordinary clock, the match programme and, most important of all, my prompt sheet. On it I would cram so much information that I reckon I could have talked live on air until midnight if I'd needed to. By the time a match kicked off on a Saturday afternoon, I probably knew more about any individual player than the wee lad's own mother. Where and when he'd been born, how many brothers and sisters he had, where he'd grown up and learned his rugby, which local school he had attended and which junior club he had started out with. That sort of thing. Then there were the little items of interest which I spent long hours searching out. I always felt that the viewers might like to have some extra information about a player they were watching; that it might enhance the pleasure they took in seeing him perform if they knew a little bit about him. So I used to go to a lot of trouble to unearth some of those facts.

Then there were the phrases which I suppose had become my stock-in-trade. It might surprise you to learn that for the most part I never prepared those. All I ever did in advance was write down the odd one or two expressions in a wee corner of my fact sheet. Similes such as 'like an animated meercat' or 'like a startled ferret'. Otherwise, they just seemed to come into my head, and I was always happy enough with that. 'They'll be celebrating in the clubhouse at Mansfield Park tonight,' just tripped off my tongue one day. Who knows where it came from. You see, in general I believed it was always a good thing to allow a little of what you might call 'emotion' into my broadcasts. If possible, I wanted people to get some sense of the wonderful atmosphere at the ground from their armchair at home. I saw it as my job to try to make the coverage as enjoyable as possible for them, and if a few evocative phrases added to their enjoyment, then I felt I had done my job. I can't remember any producer ever telling me to stop using them, so I always felt free to do so.

I didn't want anything I said to sound contrived or unreal, as if it were something I would never normally say, and to sound natural it had to be spontaneous. If it wasn't there in my mind at the right moment then it was best forgotten. Searching frantically through my papers to find a particular line I had thought up late one night while poring over my notes was not really my style. I liked to try to make my commentaries flow and I wasn't sure they would do that if I was relying too much on scripted material. Yes, I wanted my prompt sheet with me – I wouldn't go anywhere without it – but in practice, I reckon I probably used only 5 per cent of what was on it. Most of the information was there just in case I needed it. I preferred to talk about what was happening in front of me and, more importantly, in front of the viewers.

I was sad and a little apprehensive about the decision I had made to retire. But I was seventy-seven and had had a wonderful innings. Being able to do something you love for a living for only a handful of years is a privilege; I had been lucky enough to commentate for the BBC for half a century, an extraordinary length of time, and I felt I needed to go while they still wanted me. Truth to tell, I feared the tap on the shoulder in a quiet moment, and the dreaded words, 'Sorry, Bill, we've got someone else and we'd like him to do it now.' I never wanted to experience that. I wanted to finish on my terms. It was important to me that I could hold my head up and say that I had walked away from it, and not been pushed. That really would have been a sad ending.

And the travelling had become tiring. Moreover, leaving my beloved Hawick, never easy at any time in my life, had become increasingly difficult. I'd found that as you get older, you want to stay at home more often; you're not so keen to go tearing around.

It is understandable, a part of the ageing process.

All this was on my mind as I got ready for the last international match I would report. Yet I was calm, as well prepared as ever and ready to go. Contrary to what you might think, I was not especially emotional about it. At least, I wasn't until something completely unexpected happened and totally threw me and my careful preparation.

I was fiddling about with some papers, not really listening to the stadium announcements prior to the two teams coming out on to the field in three or four minutes' time. But suddenly I became aware of huge cheering and clapping coming from the by now capacity crowd. I glanced up to see that everyone in the ground was standing up and applauding. It was a remarkable sight. I peered forward to check who had come on to the pitch. Perhaps it was a famous former Welsh international arriving to take a bow. Simultaneously, I heard the voice of the stadium announcer. 'Today is Bill McLaren's final commentary for BBC Television, after a long, distinguished career of more than fifty years.' As I gazed out across the famous ground, it seemed that everyone was looking up towards where I was sitting, waving and smiling. The applause coming up from below was a lovely sound. Before I had a chance to take it in, the band was striking up 'For He's a Jolly Good Fellow', and the whole crowd, Welsh and Scots, were singing their hearts out.

Little did I know at the time that my wife Bette, daughter Linda and granddaughter Lindsay were in a BBC box which they had the honour of sharing with Tanni Grey-Thompson. They told me afterwards that by the end of the song, all four of them had tears rolling down their cheeks. I was thrilled to hear that a heroine such as Tanni was so touched by the occasion, but my goodness me, I'm glad I wasn't there with them. I'd have cracked up, I think.

As it was, I could hardly think, let alone hear anything in my headphones. The emotion of it all had suddenly washed right over me in that moment. My eyes welled up with tears, I felt my face going bright red and, I can tell you, the goose pimples were sitting up all over my body. I didn't know what to say, where to look or what to do. I was thoroughly moved by it, I don't mind admitting, and I had to wipe away a tear or two. There was a friendly, comforting hand on my shoulder, I have no idea whose.

There was, briefly, a real danger that I might dissolve into tears, and I certainly couldn't afford to do that with an international match about to start.

So I bit my bottom lip hard to try to stem the rush of thoughts and memories that were flooding through my mind.

Until that moment, I don't think it had really sunk in, but now it finally came home to me that this was it, the end. No longer would I be sitting up here, looking out on to an international ground, microphone in hand and ready to go, awaiting the studio producer's direction. No more Thursday-afternoon or Friday-morning training sessions watching players. No more experiencing the exciting build-up to an international match, a special sensation I had never tired of, even after fifty years. It was all over for me.

It wasn't easy, but I managed to regain my composure relatively quickly. Then, in no time at all, I heard that familiar voice in my earpiece and the instruction that had launched all those many commentaries.

'Cue Bill.'

CHAPTER 2
THE WORLD CUP

THE NEXT TIME I FELT THE SAME EMOTION, I WAS SITTING at home in front of my own TV set, with the trees and hills above the town of Hawick visible through the window.

It was winter 2003 and, for the first time in fifty years, the International Championship was starting without me. I was, for a moment, moved to despair. I thought to myself, 'What have you done? You've given away one of the things you have most enjoyed in all your life. What a fool you've been.'

I gather that the withdrawal symptoms suffered by heroin addicts trying to come off the drug are commonly known as 'cold turkey'. Well, I can tell you, that first Six Nations Championship in which I was not involved was my 'cold turkey'. I literally craved a role.

The whole week leading up to the first match was

a strange one for me. I seemed, suddenly, to be on the outside looking in, and I found it hard to take. Watching England completing their Grand Slam with a magnificent 42–6 victory over a hitherto unbeaten Ireland at Lansdowne Road brought it home to me just what I was missing. The trouble was, my heart was still in my job.

It was impossible to bring down the shutters abruptly on something that had been such an important part of my life for so long. I don't believe anyone could just suddenly cut themselves off from a favoured occupation after fifty years, turn their back and walk away without a pang of regret or a thought about what might have been.

Later in 2003 came the Rugby World Cup, and renewed thoughts of what might have been. This time they were all the sharper since I'd been given the opportunity to be a part of it. I had been invited to go to Australia for what would have been one last job as a commentator by BBC Radio Five Live, who asked me if I would come out of retirement and work for them. I was tempted. In fact, it was a bit more than that. I was close to agreeing to go – until I thought seriously about the travel and began to calculate what would be involved. It was not only the long flights to Australia and back but the rushing from

Perth to Sydney, and then on to Melbourne, and up to Brisbane, for individual matches. Because in Australia, it goes without saying, the distances are huge. It isn't like hopping on a plane from London to Paris and landing forty-five minutes or so later. I realised that the travelling would be probably too much for me. Then I thought about the standards I had set over the years. Was there a danger of compromising them? That was the last thing I wanted to do. I knew I could do the job, but would I do it to my own satisfaction? That uncertainty was the deciding factor. I turned down the offer, and I am glad now that I did.

That was not to say that my commentating days were over. Oh, no. This time, though, only my dear wife heard my performance. To amuse myself, just for a bit of fun, for some of the games I turned down the sound behind the ITV pictures and gave the commentary I would have delivered had I been there myself working for the independent channel. Not that there was ever any likelihood of that, although before my retirement I had had two or three approaches from ITV to do rugby commentary for World Cups. I never even considered it. In my heart, I was always too much of a BBC man to be tempted, even though it probably would have meant being able to work at all four previous Rugby World Cups.

But I never forgot that it was the BBC who had supported me for years and years, and how fair they had been in the way they treated me. I liked and respected the people I worked with there and I was always very comfortable with my relationship with the corporation. So when ITV came calling, there was never any great decision to be made.

Of course, it would have been good to have been in the swim again at the 2003 World Cup. It was always a challenge I relished to get to the ground with all my preparations made, and then, some hours later, savouring the greatest joy of all: reaching the end of the game, hearing the final whistle and thinking to yourself, 'Thank God that commentary seemed to go well!' But I am philosophical enough to realise that all good things come to an end. So instead I settled down to conduct my careful study of the tournament at home. It promised much and, I am delighted to say, generally speaking, it delivered a great deal. The Australian people supported the event magnificently, turning out at every location in numbers that absolutely thrilled the organisers. Matches between a couple of the minnows of the world game, Canada against Tonga at Wollongong, say, attracted five-figure audiences, which was a wonderful tribute to the enthusiasm of the Australian folk.

When Romania met Namibia in Launceston, Tasmania, the local mayor decreed that anyone living in a house with an odd number would support Namibia and those in an even-numbered home would barrack for Romania, as they say in Australia. It was a great idea and brought a real party atmosphere to the occasion.

Generally speaking, Rugby World Cup 2003 was a great tournament. It was well run, marvellously supported and created immense interest among sports-minded people all around the world. It is a pretty good vehicle for rugby to show its wares, and I don't think the game does badly out of it. Even in the one-sided games, you get some lovely fluent football played, with the ball twinkling through the hands. And that shows the minor countries what can be achieved by slick ball transference. And the best side won the cup, which is always preferable. England at last played to their potential and it was great for the northern hemisphere to have somebody up there among the hot-shots of the world game. Of course, I wish it had been Scotland, but as that was never on the cards I was delighted to see England take the trophy. They won it well, and the whole northern hemisphere had reason to be chuffed, because it was some feat.

Naturally the victory made England the target for all teams, as they were throughout the 2004 Six Nations Championship, where they finished third in the table behind France, who achieved the Grand Slam, and Ireland, who took the Triple Crown. They were under more huge pressure in June, when they made a short tour of New Zealand and Australia, having beaten both countries, 15–13 in Wellington and 25–14 in Melbourne respectively, a year earlier in the run-up to the World Cup. By then it was obvious that England's World Cup-winning side had long since broken up. England found that the new side they took down to the southern hemisphere was not strong enough to cope with the All Blacks and Wallabies, both of whom were keen to take the scalp of the new world champions. England lost twice in New Zealand and also to Australia in Brisbane. But I am not sure we should read too much into those results.

England had begun the rebuilding phase and new players always take time to slot in. Also, other key players such as Lawrence Dallaglio and Richard Hill had been playing rugby virtually non-stop for a year. They must have been weary making a tour like that at the end of a domestic season which included the World Cup. I sometimes think that in the modern game we ask too much of our finest players.

One surprising aspect of the 2003 World Cup was how much punting of the ball there was. There were times when I had the feeling we were drifting back to the 1950s, when players used the punt far too often as an easy option, and to offset tight, flat-lying defences. I wondered whether we were putting boot to ball too much instead of allowing the ball to go through the hands. It seemed to me that so many of the real contests were settled by kicks rather than tries. I just hope the top teams will set the tone of attacking rugby with handling as the key ingredient when the next World Cup takes place.

Too many of the early pool matches were one-sided and I would try to adjust the format with that in mind. When a team loses by sixty or eighty points we tend to draw the conclusion that the match has been a total failure, and there is no doubt that the sort of score which Australia ran up against Namibia in Adelaide (142–0), or the 111 points England amassed against Uruguay, damages the game. Yet sometimes the team at the wrong end of such a score is delighted just to be out on the same pitch as one of the big guns. So we have to be careful we don't eliminate countries from the World Cup merely because they have taken a huge beating. It would be a pity to exclude some of the smaller fry altogether. Perhaps instead they could be included in a separate section for the minor rugby-playing nations, or there could be some kind of eliminating contest before the main event gets under way. I suppose, from a positive point of view, you could say that if you don't learn from playing against Australia or England, there is something wrong with you, and I guess the smaller nations are bound to take important lessons away with them from those meetings. Ideally, in future World Cups, I would like to see those one-sided scorelines disappearing. It would mean the smaller nations were getting stronger, a good sign of the growth of the sport worldwide. The heavyweights of the world game will always come out on top, as they do in soccer. For example, how often have countries like Brazil, Argentina, Germany and Italy won the soccer World Cup? More often than not, is the truth.

I thought Australia did marvellously well. They came so close to snatching the cup, and always victory over New Zealand deserves a pat on the back. It is very seldom you find a weak New Zealand side, and to beat them in the semi-final in so overwhelming a manner was a terrific achievement for Australia. My feeling is that the All Blacks will always be there or thereabouts. Generally, as they showed in the year leading up to the tournament, the New Zealanders know what they are doing and how to play a vibrant brand of rugby football. It was their misfortune that they got it wrong just when it mattered most: in the semi-final of the World Cup.

I have to say I am surprised they have not won the World Cup since I saw them do it on their home territory in the very first tournament in 1987. You would not expect New Zealand to go twenty years between World Cup wins, but in fact that is the shortest possible interval since they won't have another chance until 2007. However, perhaps that statistic is more a reflection of how other countries have caught up with New Zealand and become so much more competitive than they used to be than an indication of any problem within New Zealand rugby. Australia in particular have played some wonderful football in those intervening years, and I suspect that South Africa are a better side than their record suggests. The southern hemisphere nations will always set standards which we in the British Isles will have to work hard to match. That is the way of the rugby-playing world. And in the northern hemisphere, England will always be the main challengers because they have the mix now of power up front and gifted back play. In years to come, it would be my fervent wish that when the northern hemisphere sides take on their counterparts from the southern hemisphere, they achieve a better average of wins than in the past.

Some expressed their disappointment with what Scotland achieved, but I did not share that view. We did as well as we might have expected. We are a small country with wee resources and our successes will come only occasionally. We held our own to finish in the last eight, and we have to be satisfied with that. I am not saying we cannot do better, because maybe we can. But we have to build an element of realism into our calculations. Overall, I felt our performance in Australia was fairly good. We beat Fiji to reach the quarter-final, and they are never a pushover. It was no disgrace, either, to lose to Australia there, for they went on to defeat New Zealand and came desperately close to toppling England in the final.

For me as a commentator, World Cups were just hard graft in terms of remembering names. You really have to slog because you are dealing with so many players that you have never seen before, and all you have is a bit of background information. And when it came to countries like Western Samoa or

Tonga, it's not just a question of remembering names, you have to remember how to pronounce them, too.

I covered the inaugural World Cup in 1987 in Australia and New Zealand, a rugby land I have always admired. I saw so many wonderful, powerful rugby men come out of that country that I refuse to accept the New Zealanders are no longer capable of producing world-class players in all positions. It can be a harsh country in terms of its climate and geography, and exhausting to navigate when you are there to watch rugby. You always seem to be flying in or out of somewhere: from Auckland to Hamilton, Wellington to Dunedin or Christchurch. And that 1987 visit, of course, also involved crossing back and forth from Australia. The distances to be travelled are nothing like as great as those in Australia, but you are still flying a great deal. I remember being frozen in on the South Island once. The local airport was closed for a spell and there was no option but to wait for the cold snap to ease. So it can be a tough country to tour.

Yet it is a marvellous place from the rugby point of view, because everybody there talks about the game. So even though it is on the other side of the world, it feels very much like a home from home; very like Hawick, where rugby is the main topic of conversation among many folk. That sense of familiarity is emphasised by the landscape. Parts of New Zealand, with its rivers, streams, hills and trees, remind me so much of Scotland. And not without reason is Dunedin, at the southern tip of the South Island, known as the Edinburgh of the southern hemisphere.

I took the chance to see some of the country while I was there in 1987, though I could not appreciate it to the full because I had to concentrate on the job I was there to do. I felt the strain of trying to do my commentaries as well as I possibly could, only too aware that in New Zealand, of all places, where youngsters grow up almost tied to a rugby ball, I had to be spot-on. With so many experts on the game all around me, I felt under huge pressure to perform to the best of my ability. Their standards were high, and mine had to be, too. They wouldn't have been if I had spent too long gazing at mountains or relaxing beside beautiful lakes in the winter sunshine, however attractive that prospect might have been.

I will always remember the semi-final of that World Cup, between Australia and France, which was hosted by Australia in Sydney. It was a sheer delight of a match, won dramatically at the end by the French when Serge Blanco, the wonderfully charismatic full-back, raced into the corner for the winning score. I found it challenging working in both countries in what were to me alien environments. It was always a problem getting to see teams training when you were travelling so much, and that affected the amount of 'homework' I was able to do and made it harder to identify players in an instant, which was very frustrating. I was also less of a familiar face in the southern hemisphere, and people are inevitably suspicious of those they don't know or recognise. So it was very different from operating in the Home Nations Championship, where most people knew who I was and what I was there to do.

One man I came across at that World Cup and liked a great deal was the Australian coach, Alan Jones. He was forthright and blunt, to say the least, but he knew what he wanted and what he was about. His was certainly a different style from what I was accustomed to back home, and indeed it irritated many people, but I found it refreshing. He may have been sharp, very to the point, and he called a spade a spade, but he knew his rugby inside out and he was prepared to air his views. He could never have been accused of shying away from TV cameras. I thought he was very helpful to those of us 'in the trade', and one of the great characters in rugby.

He was one of the most knowledgeable of them, too.

That World Cup had thrown up an extraordinary result in the quarter-final, when England went to Brisbane heavily favoured to defeat a Welsh team wracked by injuries. Wales had to call up a young, inexperienced front-row forward named David Young to shore up their scrummage. No one gave them a chance. Maybe the fact that they had nothing to lose was why they won easily, 16–3. That result remains one of the biggest ever upsets in World Cup history.

England had seemed too strong on paper, and too well prepared, to succumb to a struggling Wales. But as so often, they flattered to deceive. They were a huge disappointment in that tournament and subsided meekly. It was somehow typical of English international rugby at that time. So many English sides never realised their potential, yet they had some fine players, people like Wade Dooley and Peter Winterbottom up front and Jamie Salmon behind the scrum. Salmon was a very clever player, and a nice guy, too. He had been good enough to represent the All Blacks, something you only did in those days if you were a player out of the very top drawer. In later years, I ran across Jamie Salmon again when he was doing bits of commentary, and I was very impressed with his work. I think he is one of the best commentators in the business because he is down to earth, very knowledgeable and does not try to blind people with science. Most important of all, his recognition of players is especially good. Not all present-day commentators can claim all those attributes.

New Zealand won that first World Cup and justifiably so. In David Kirk, their scrum-half and captain, they had a snappy little player who was also an option-taker. He was very aware of situations, a real bright spark who provided a quality service for Grant Fox, their goal-kicking outside-half who, as an orthodox stand-off half, performed the basics superbly well.

Wing John Kirwan was a huge force, as was Joe Stanley, one of the centres inside him. It seemed that wherever you looked in that All Black side, there was power and purpose. Gallagher was a livewire, attacking full-back who came into the back line at a real lick and whose choice of offensive angle and route was spot-on. In my view it was Gallagher who popularised full-back intrusion into the line. Michael Jones, a flanker who hunted opponents like a jaguar, was at that time the best openside flank forward in the world. It was no great surprise, then, that New

Zealand became the first country to lift the William Webb Ellis trophy.

To be at that inaugural World Cup was to sense the dawn of a new sporting adventure. In truth, it wasn't the most organised sporting tournament ever known, and I don't think in the end any money was made for the IRB. But a World Cup is a World Cup, and it was a start. Since then, it has grown in stature as a great world event.

In the second World Cup, hosted jointly by Britain, Ireland and France in 1991, I felt that England threw away the trophy. Mystifyingly, they changed the way they had played previously for the final at Twickenham, and of course jeopardised everything in doing so. To play the wide, expansive game they sought to produce in the final required much practice, yet they clearly believed they could switch styles overnight. Up to that point, they had played a tight, forward-orientated game throughout the tournament and for the life of me I will never understand why they suddenly abandoned that approach for a high-risk game. They had a superb combination at lock forward in Wade Dooley and Paul Ackford, and in Mike Teague they had a hugely underrated workhorse of a player. He may have looked more like a prop than a loose forward but few could match his strength and support work in the loose. It had been a joy to see such a powerful pack producing such high-quality rugby, even if they did use it to beat Scotland 9–6 in the semi-final at Murrayfield. And behind that pack, they had in Rob Andrew the perfect man to channel and direct their whole game with his shrewd kicking into the corners and the sheer variety of his play. Andrew was a fine player, and I admired him greatly.

Had they not changed styles, I am sure England would have won. To revolutionise their entire game plan in a World Cup final suggested to me that they needed their heads examined. Given what had gone before in that tournament, it must rank as practically the most disappointing display ever by an England team.

Instead Australia won the Cup for the first time, and in David Campese they had not only the player of the tournament but my own particular favourite from all my years of watching the game. David could revive a match that was faltering. I so admired that willingness to tilt his lance, to have a go, not to be tied down, but to play as he felt was right. When I saw him direct the ball to the perfect spot to create a crucial try for Tim Horan against New Zealand in the semi-final in Dublin, I could hardly believe my eyes. Better still, he also scored himself, suddenly popping up in the fly-half position and taking the ball from a ruck before cutting a clever angle on the outside break to race into the corner beyond the grasp of the New Zealand defenders. For me, 'Campo' was the greatest entertainer of the lot and yet, when he was running, he didn't give the impression of lightning speed. It was his change of pace that was so devastating. As a commentator, I would rather cover Campese with the ball in his hands than any other player I have seen. His ability to light up the scene made it a sheer delight to report on him.

He has been accused of deliberately knocking on late on in the final to prevent Rory Underwood from receiving the ball when he appeared to have a clear run to the Australian line. But I have to say I thought it was an unintentional knock-on, not an infringement that deserved the penalty try called for by some. Having said that, it did deny England the rare opportunity of a clear two-on-one situation. And with Underwood's pace, there was every chance he'd have got to the Australian line.

Generally, in 1991 I felt that English rugby still lacked a spark, that electricity the great attacking sides produce. The England forwards over the years had always been formidable but their backs disappointed time and again and didn't reach their true potential often enough. When you think of some of the outstanding backs England have turned out – players like Dickie Jeeps, Jeff Butterfield and Richard Sharp in the 1950s and 1960s, David Duckham and Keith Fielding going into the 1970s, John Carleton and Jamie Salmon in the 1980s and Jeremy Guscott in the 1990s – you have to scratch your head in amazement that they achieved so little for so long. Now, of course, it is different, but for decades England underachieved.

Part of the reason for England's failure to fulfil their potential is the fact that the mere sight of them makes the opposition roll up their sleeves and look to their laurels. That was certainly the case with both Wales in the quarter-final of the 1987 World Cup, and Australia in the 1991 final. But another factor was that England seemed to see themselves as a successful side before they actually were one. The best example of that was the 1990 Grand Slam show-down with Scotland at Murrayfield, when England clearly thought the game was in the bag before they even started. A determined Scottish team set out to prove otherwise and had a day to remember as a result. When victory proved altogether harder to attain than England had assumed, they lost their way.

Nevertheless, England have always been the side to beat among the four home unions. Wales and Ireland have had their moments, Ireland most recently in coming second to France in the 2004 Six Nations Championship, ahead of England, and in the 2003 World Cup, where they should have defeated Australia to set up a quarter-final clash with Scotland. The chance slipped through their fingers on that occasion, as had the opportunity to snatch a rare Grand Slam when they met England in the final game of the Six Nations Championship that year. Wales, of course, had their glory years during the 1970s. Yet England have remained the pacemakers. I am sure the Scots would rather beat them than anyone else. Part of that is down to our age-old rivalry, but it is also because they are a hell of a good side. They deserved their World Cup win.

In 1995 it was South Africa's World Cup, from every point of view. It was an emotional event, characterised by the presence of Nelson Mandela in the wings, willing on the team that represented what he termed the 'Rainbow Nation'. Many felt, though, that New Zealand played the best rugby of the tournament, and certainly in the way their team, so inspired by the extraordinary Jonah Lomu, overran England in the semi-final, there was a case to prosecute on that score. It was surprising that the other semi-final, between South Africa and France, was even played that night in Durban, for the heavens opened and saturated the pitch. I think the entire rugby world will for ever remember that famous image of a dozen local women trying to sweep the water off the surface at King's Park with brooms.

Yet winning World Cups is often a matter of which players can best handle the pressures and expectations on the day. South Africa, just as England were to do in Australia in 2003 through Jonny Wilkinson, won with a dropped goal by their fly-half late in extra time. On that occasion it was Joel Stransky who delivered the goods for his country.

In 1999, another South African no. 10, Jannie de Beer, also made an amazing contribution to the tournament when he landed an extraordinary five dropped goals to end England's hopes in the quarter-finals in Paris. Players like the great Frenchman Pierre Albaladejo of Dax and France, the man they called 'Monsieur Le Drop', managed two or even three in a game from time to time, but five in one match was absolutely remarkable. I had never seen anything like it, and nor had England, judging from the shell-shocked expressions on their faces as they trooped off the field at the end. But then, dropping a goal is a relatively easy way for a rugby player to earn points if he has practised the technique long enough. It is a device that can be mastered by working at it endlessly, which is what players like De Beer and Wilkinson did. Nor is it a modern trick. I remember a pre-war player named W.C.W. Murdoch, of Hillhead High School Former Pupils, knocking over three dropped goals in a Scottish club match.

The 1999 World Cup was not one of the greatest. Defences dominated, and the team with the tightest defence, Australia, under coach Rod McQueen, emerged to take the trophy, beating France in the final. Undoubtedly the match of the tournament was the semi-final in which France came from behind to stun the All Blacks at Twickenham with the type of handling and running that probably only a French side could produce collectively, at such an unexpected moment. It simply bewildered and overwhelmed the All Blacks, dazzling and delighting in the process observers of neutral disposition.

The World Cup has been wonderful for the game worldwide. It has helped rugby find countless numbers of new supporters, in once unknown rugby-playing countries as well as in the established nations, and served up some pulsating games rich in entertainment. The best sides may not always have won the crunch games, but isn't that the nature of cup matches everywhere? Without the element of unpredictability that induces the excitement so essential to sport, I doubt whether the event would have been half as successful.

CHAPTER 3
A VISION OF HELL ON EARTH

THERE WAS ONE FIXTURE I WASN'T KEEN TO ATTEND. IT is one that is remembered by millions of others all around the world, and it was not a match I would even have wanted to commentate on, never mind participate in. The Allies v. The Axis, 1939–45. Venue: almost the entire globe.

But there I was, in northern Italy, early one morning in 1944, just after the sun had come up, leading a group of men on a forward reconnaissance. I was looking for a gun position, which was one of my duties as a forward observance officer. As we came into a small town, we quickly became aware of a peculiar smell. It was a very strong, sweet, sickly sort of smell, and it seemed to fill the air. As it was winter, we could discount the scent of overripe flowers wafting on the breeze. Any old soldiers will already have a good idea of the source of this cloying stench.

We moved carefully towards what had been the town centre. No one seemed to be about. There were no children standing on the street corners, as there often were when the British Army passed through a town or village; no adults hovering, the weariness and brutality of war etched in the furrows across their foreheads. In fact, there didn't seem to be a living soul there. All we could see was destruction: buildings bombed and shattered, broken-down and wrecked vehicles lying in the streets.

In the middle of the town, we turned a corner and saw a graveyard. What confronted me there was a sight that remains with me sixty years later. There must have been, piled up on the ground within this one cemetery, around 1,500 dead Germans and Italians. The bodies lay there in their death throes, grotesquely contorted, one on top of the other and four or five deep. Both the smell and this nightmare vision were indescribable. Many of the corpses had had limbs blown off; there were men and women without feet or arms, children with legs missing. It was the most horrific thing I had ever seen in my life, indeed ever would see. I was twenty-one years old.

Apparently, the Germans had put down a huge barrage and had hit the village, accidentally, it was said. But, once it was taken, they had dug in and, some time later, confronted the advancing British Army. There had been an absolute bloodbath. Local men, women and children, as was all too vividly evident, had been caught up in the battle and had paid a terrible price. The Germans, too, had been wiped out and their corpses lay strewn in heaps in this cemetery along with those of the townsfolk.

I had seen dead bodies before since arriving in Italy, but nothing on this horrifying scale. Somehow, this pitiless slaughter seemed to encapsulate the greater conflict into which we had been dragged. It was a glimpse of hell on earth, and we were right in the middle of it, watching our chums, our enemies and innocent civilians alike losing their lives right in front of us.

Here were simple people, leading ordinary, decent lives, suddenly thrust into terrible violence which snuffed out those lives in an instant. And now here they were in their own cemetery, not decently buried after a natural death but thrown on top of one another, innocent victims of war. For weeks afterwards, I could not get that shocking image out of my mind, nor the stench of decaying bodies out of my nostrils. Even today, I can still picture the scene with an awful clarity. It was an experience that underlined the horror and futility of war, and also one that turned youths into men. You matured pretty quickly when you were exposed to such brutalities.

When you grow old, you look back on your life and reflect upon key stages, specific moments. That day in 1944 in Italy was certainly one of those key moments for me. I have never forgotten, and I never will. When I was a youngster, rugby football was everything in the world to me. But when I left my home at that early age and faced terrible scenes like that, it rocked my world to its foundations. Suddenly I was forced to realise that the world can be a horrific place and that there are some terrible people in it. But what can you do, other than follow your orders and do your duty? There was no questioning it, no time to think about it. You did as you were told, and beyond that, you acted on your instincts. Mankind has a sort of inbuilt self-preservation mechanism, and in times of danger, that takes over.

I had been called up in 1942 at the age of eighteen. Of course, the war seemed a long way away from my home in the beautiful Scottish Borders. In Hawick we heard no sound of explosions, no guns booming. There was an amateurishly organised local defence force but, from what I can remember, not much else. Yet it was impossible not to be aware of what was going on in the wider world, and I honestly wanted to do my bit to help my country and defend the life I knew.

So once my call-up papers had arrived, I set my mind to the task ahead. There was a job to be done and we had to get on with it. There were no two ways about it: you just accepted what had to be and prepared yourself as best you could for whatever might lie ahead. But few of us young lads could possibly have had any idea of what it would be like once we reached the war zone and encountered actual fighting.

I went first to the big army camp at Catterick in north Yorkshire for about six weeks of what they euphemistically called 'initial training'. What that actually meant was a legalised beating-up. They just knocked the hell out of you, in true Army style, in the hope that by the end of it you would understand and accept discipline and be in some sort of reasonable physical shape to handle what was to come. You never went outside the camp to socialise or meet any-one else, and once your initiation was over, your cheeks had sunk into your face and you had a raw, hungry, mean look about you. I suppose they reasoned that even if we couldn't kill hundreds of Germans single-handed, just by looking so bloody grim and frightening (most of the hair on our heads had been shaved off), we might persuade a few to surrender if we got close enough.

Delicate, hitherto protected young men with sheltered upbringings found themselves subjected to indignities and exertions they could never have imagined even in their worst nightmares. Forced marches through the night, shouted orders, roared-out reprimands, privations. It bore little resemblance to the lifestyles most of us had known until then. I was luckier than some because I'd been used to the fitness levels demanded by Hawick Rugby Club and to the need, in a sporting context, to follow orders. All right, Hawick RFC wasn't quite the Army, but even so, rugby training had made me a lot fitter than most of my new chums. And although we'd had a lot of fun at Hawick and indulged in a lot of horseplay – pouring cold water over guys in the showers and that sort of thing – we'd also had it drummed into us, usually by Tom Wright, a stern disciplinarian who used to take training, that we had to work at being fit, hard and determined to win matches.

So the Army fitness training didn't worry me too much. Mind you, it was no cakewalk when we found ourselves in some murky stream, up to our necks in water and carrying saturated packs on our backs, trying to wade through the current with our rifles held high above our heads. If you allowed your gun to get wet, you were really for it. We would be made to crawl through muddy culverts, or under barbed-wire fences, again keeping our rifles in good shape. One or two guys found it quite tough surviving. It was hardly surprising: if you had been used to working in a bank, say, you wouldn't be prepared in any way for these physical challenges, executed to a background cacophony of Army sergeants shouting orders at you at the top of their voices. We were taken pretty near to the edge of our endurance, for the Army knew how to test you, all right. You were absolutely shattered at the end of some of those days.

The Army is unique in the way it plunges you into a veritable maelstrom of human beings, people from all walks of life, many of whom you would never have associated with in your entire lives on Civvy Street. But once in Army fatigues, you had to mix with all types and get on with them. These might be the men you would be fighting alongside, and you might need to rely on them to save your life. I remember one chap, Willie was his name, from the west of Scotland. He was a laid-back fellow who operated at his own pace, and nothing fazed him. He seemed immune to the Army's attempts to make a soldier of him. If he felt like reading a newspaper when the rest of us were working, that's what he would do. He just sauntered through the training, driving the sergeant-major to distraction. Willie would stand calmly on the parade ground, looking all innocent, having been hauled out for some misdemeanour, while the sergeant-major bawled at him. He seemed to be half-asleep most of the time.

The Army was about teamwork, so there was a fellowship that was built up cleverly by those in charge. But you were open-mouthed with shock half the time at what they expected you to do. Yet there were men you respected. We had a company sergeant-major, Sergeant-Major Fell, who was an absolute tyrant, a real hard case, but I thought the world of him. He was the perfect example of what a British soldier should be: supremely fit, strong and clear-minded. In fact, he was so fit he looked in need of a good meal. He was an inspiring character and I would have done anything to be part of his troop. There was never any nastiness or viciousness about him, but he knew precisely what he wanted to achieve and made sure all his men went for it, whatever physical pain was involved. He would tell people off when it was merited, yet somehow he managed to motivate them, driving them to reach higher standards than they would ever have imagined themselves capable of attaining.

At Catterick, it was apparently decided – God knows how – that I might be officer material, so I was then transferred to a camp in the south of England, Wrotham, in Kent, which ran a special officer cadet training course.

At Wrotham, a most revealing, in-depth conversation took place. It went something like this:

'Was your father in the last war?'

'Yes, sir.'

'What branch was he in?'

'In the artillery, sir.'

'Right, you'll be in the artillery.'

'Thank you, sir.'

And that was how I became 2nd Lieutenant 281771, Royal Artillery.

Next I was posted to an officer training camp in Staffordshire, at Alton Towers, today, of course, the site of the huge amusement park. Well, I can tell you, it wasn't so amusing in those days. In fact, we were confronted by death almost straight away. We returned to our billet on the top floor of the main building one day to hear that one of our pals had been found dead at the foot of the building. It seemed he had fallen out of a window, although whether he may have jumped, no one knew. Like most of us, he was just a wee lad in his late teens, away from his home for the first time. That pulled me up pretty short. I began to understand very quickly that this was where the real world began, and that my warm, comfortable childhood was already far behind me.

Part of our officer training was doubtless designed to discover what any of us had in the way of essential grey matter floating around in our heads. So we would be set devilish tasks like being woken up by explosions and thunderflashes in the middle of the night in our tents in some bleak part of the country we'd never set foot in before, and ordered to find our way back to the camp headquarters. Quite apart from knowing nothing about your surroundings, you would be completely disorientated by the rude awakening, and, of course, it was pitch black and freezing cold. But you had to start thinking fast about the way to go and what to do. Oh, and you daren't lose any of their precious bloody Army equipment en route, either. Leave something out on some remote moorland, and they would send you back to find it, even if it was still dark.

We would be made to wriggle across open land while under 'enemy' fire, with live bullets zipping over our heads, and to survive being dunked in the icy sea. Once you go into the water in those temperatures, there is a risk that your capacity for rational thought will break down within two minutes. You cannot remember where you are, what you are supposed to be doing or, in the worst cases, even your own serial number. I have since seen television documentaries in which Army recruits are subjected to this kind of legalised brutality, and if you're sitting in your comfy armchair at home beside a warm fire, it is highly entertaining watching some poor wee lad, soaked to the skin and frozen to the bone, become so disorientated he is struggling even to remember his own name. But it's a different story if you are the poor damned fool playing the role of guinea pig.

I suppose there was method in their madness, and plainly someone was scrutinising all this and drawing some conclusion from it, because not all of us earned selection as an officer. But most managed to stumble their way through the various tortures. And the exercises did give you an idea of the tasks that might lie ahead, and an appreciation of the need to think clearly and quickly under intense stress, particularly if you were responsible for a group of men under your command.

In 1943, our eventual destination turned out to be Italy, but someone with a cracking sense of humour decided we ought to take the scenic route – via north Africa. We were shipped out from Liverpool, enjoying the dubious pleasures of a cramped troopship and wondering all the while whether at any moment a German U-boat might be lining us up in her sights, preparing to send the lot of us into oblivion. I have to say I have made more pleasurable journeys in my lifetime.

Once we arrived in north Africa, most of us became ill. Dysentery was the chief problem. That condition is not just debilitating but humiliating, too. You frequently find yourself totally at the mercy of your body and its basic functions. Your guts are heaving and the overwhelming need to seek immediate relief simply cannot be ignored. But wars don't stop for anything, so many a sick soldier was unable to reach a latrine. Defecation into clothes that had to continue to be worn was commonplace, especially in other theatres of the war, such as the Russian front. It was grim and demeaning for every soldier affected.

At least by the time we got to north Africa General Montgomery and his 8th Army had finally nailed Rommel and the world had heard of a small, innocuous railway halt named El-Alamein. It was here that one of the great battles of the whole war had been fought and the German Afrika Corps had been destroyed. It marked the end of Hitler's adventures in the desert.

From Algiers, we were sent off by train to Bizerta, a journey of around fifty or sixty hours. Our food consisted of bully-beef and spam. Nothing else. The chances of getting anything as exotic as fresh fruit and vegetables were remote. It became repetitive and unappetising after only the first few meals, but unfortunately for us, it was to be our staple diet throughout the Italian campaign. That and, of course, tea. Whenever we stopped anywhere, whether it was out in the country or in the middle of a town or city, someone would brew up. Without tea, I reckon the British Army would have been useless. It took the British squaddie through an awful lot of campaigns.

At Bizerta, we clambered into a troop-carrier for the crossing to Italy. On the long sea voyage from Liverpool to north Africa I'd been one of the few able to hold on to the contents of his stomach, but on the choppy waters we encountered now, I lost my pre-eminent position. I think it was the sight of an officer heaping marmalade on to a lump of spam which finally did it for me. Even the thought of that combination still turns my stomach. And it did a lot more than turn then, on that crude Army troop-carrier bouncing about on the rough sea.

I was to be involved in the fighting on the Italian peninsula for two whole years. Too long, that's for sure. I was attached to 20/21 Battery, 5 Medium Regiment, Royal Artillery, which I joined shortly after the Salerno landings. I soon learned that I was to be one of the officers responsible for some pretty serious firepower the Allies planned to unleash on the Germans, who were sitting right across the middle of Italy barring our path to the north. In training, we had used 25 lb guns and had been suitably impressed at the mess they could create. But when we saw what 5.5 shells could do, we realised we had moved up a league. You'd have a serious headache if you got in the path of one of those things as it smashed down anywhere near you.

But being under fire and directing fire was something I was going to have to accept during the course of the next couple of years. You couldn't say you ever got used to it, but you adapted because you had to. One day I was scouting ahead with my wireless operator, looking for a suitable site to set up our forward observation, when we suddenly became aware of incoming shells. From our own side. Apparently, they had not been informed of our mission, so when they saw movement, they opened fire. The prospect of being killed by the Germans with their accurate mortar fire was bad enough, but the idea that you might be blown to smithereens by your own men was truly appalling.

One place dominated our thinking for month after month: Monte Cassino. To anyone who remembers the Second World War or has learned even a little about it since, that name will be instantly familiar, as will the sense of dread attached to it. For it was a place where the slaughter seemed endless. The Battle of Monte Cassino would prove to be the largest land battle in Europe, the bloodiest encounter the Allies had with the Germans anywhere during the war.

Monte Cassino was the site of a Benedictine monastery dating back to AD 530, perched right on the top of a mountain halfway up Italy, overlooking the Liri Valley. In early 1944, it was completely blocking the Allied advance on Rome. It offered fantastic panoramic views right across the surrounding hills and mountains, so whoever commanded it was in pole position, as it were. Our problem was that it was the Germans, under Field-Marshal Kesselring, who were sitting up there, while we were confined to the valleys and hills below, constantly peering up at this bloody great thing. It is a wonder I and thousands of other Allied soldiers did not come home from the war with a permanent crick in our necks from staring up at that huge edifice on the top of the mountain. It got to the stage where you grew sick of the very mention of its name.

We fought for Monte Cassino through entire seasons – that was how long the siege went on – enduring climatic extremes of all kinds. In summer it was almost unbearably hot, and the dust got into everything: eyes, ears, mouth, nose, food and equipment. But when the heavy rain arrived, the ground turned to liquid mud, solidifying into snow and ice in winter. I can remember having to help the guys get their guns out of the thick, cloying mud. You had to grab the gun-carriage wheel in order to get the damned thing moving; you'd be covered in the stuff and wet through, but you just had to get the guns out. As winter set in the weather grew harsh, and you had to rely on men and mules to move equipment through snow. There was no other feasible method of doing it.

It was a stage of my life which I hardly recall fondly. Occasionally, on a beautiful, sunny, late-summer morning, in the very brief interlude between when you awoke and when the firing started, just for a moment you could almost forget you were at war and just enjoy the singing of the few birds that hadn't been blown to bits by the guns. But any pleasurable moments were few and very far between, and it was never long before the crump of shells and the booming of huge guns reminded you that you couldn't possibly be anywhere other than in the middle of a war zone.

The enemy's position seemed well-nigh impossible to breach. The Allied forces threw everything they had at the mountain fortress, but it refused to fall. The Germans were under assault from the air and from all southerly directions on the ground, but too many men were losing their lives in a series of failed attempts. In one of those, I came within two feet of losing mine.

I had come down the mountain from an observation forward command post, which was where I spent most of my war. My job was to direct our shellfire, via a field telephone, on to enemy positions across the valley or in the hills. You often had to crawl for a couple of hundred yards on your belly, with a telephone cable trailing behind you, just to get to the site where you were going to set up your observation post. You had to take care not to stir up any dust because that would tell the Germans where you were and what you were doing and they would pour down fire on you. Often your position would come under attack, but what I loathed most about being up there was that you were virtually on your own. You had an assistant, a lance-bombardier who helped to link the telephone cable, but once you were actually up in the observation post, looking through your binoculars to see where the Germans were, it was scary. Especially at night, when all kinds of strange sounds fed your imagination. You had no idea what was going on around you, and the enemy might well have spotted you and decided to creep up under cover of darkness to launch a surprise raid. So you got very little sleep. A bit on and off, but nothing extensive. You had to endure this for four or five days at a stretch. Someone brought your food from behind, or sometimes your lance-bombardier went down to collect it.

I had an enormous amount of respect for the ordinary soldiers involved in hand-to-hand fighting with the Germans. I remember once having to report from my forward observation post on how the big guns' fire had fared against its target before the 2nd Hampshire Regiment moved forward. The barrage went down all right but there were some stray shells about. That didn't stop the Hampshires. They kept fighting their way up the hill even though there were still Germans sitting on the top. When the Germans chased them off, the Hampshires simply went back up the hill. Again they were chased off. But on their third attempt they finally took the hill. They were magnificent, the Hampshires, time and again. I was sitting in the forward observation post watching most of this through my binoculars. You could see men being hit and killed, and others being injured and crawling away. I could only sit there with my knees knocking. It was like a grandstand seat in front of the fighting. You just had to accept whatever your role was and stick with it.

That was the great thing about the British Army: they muddled through somehow. They had clear targets and they wouldn't be diverted from them; nor would they be satisfied until they had achieved their objective. But chief among the soldiers, I'll never forget those brave infantry guys.

The night of my brush with death I had to go on an operation with an infantry outfit. They wanted an artillery officer with them to look right down into the German lines from the top of a hill and recommend a position for another observation post. I went with my lance-bombardier, who was carrying his length of telephone wire. It was quiet at the time, as there was hardly any firing. So there we were with this little infantry unit, them in front, us behind trailing out our telephone line, which was making a 'tick, tick,

tick' sound as it rolled off the reel. I was so scared. The noise sounded positively deafening to me in the silence and I was sure the Germans would be able to hear and might suddenly open up.

At the crest of the hill we found a little indentation that was ideal for our observation post. We were organising ourselves when I realised we had left something behind. I said I'd go back to collect it. As I made my way carefully down again, suddenly the silence of the night was broken by a loud 'Sheeeeeoow!' The sound whizzed by my ear and the silence returned. I knew at once what it was, and if I'd been in any doubt, the impact of the bullet hitting the ground just a couple of feet away from me would have confirmed it. A sniper, using night-sights, had trailed me down the hill for a moment and then taken aim. The bullet had literally fizzed past me before burying itself in the ground. I was unscathed. Two feet further to the right, and I would probably have been dead. Such is the thin dividing line between life and death.

It became clear that this particular German sniper had taken out quite a few of our boys. Imagine our pleasure, then, a few days later, when news came back that the advancing Allied infantry had caught up with him and silenced him for ever.

I had not personally taken anyone's life, although of course I was indirectly responsible for enemy deaths by pinpointing targets for our guns. That narrow escape emphasised to me the stupidity of one guy killing another when he had nothing at all against him. But it had to be done. Everyone had a job to do. It was a matter of duty; it was what you were there for. I had no compunction about what my messages back via the field telephone would mean for the ordinary German soldiers I could see through my binoculars walking around in their camp, or crawling into look-out positions further up the mountain. Within a short time of my message being received, either our huge guns would fire at them, or, eventually, Allied aircraft would appear in the sky, taking turns on their bombing runs to pound the enemy positions in and around the hills. You were raining down death on these human beings, but you couldn't be squeamish about it. For, as the incident with the German sniper had made clear, it was either them or you. Someone was going to win, and someone had to lose.

The moral issue became more difficult to resolve when we knew there were Germans hiding in a local village. Their highly trained snipers would sometimes take up positions in buildings used by civilians, or their artillery would set up in the middle of a place where ordinary people were living. Of course, in those circumstances, you could show no mercy to the civilians. We would put down a barrage that might flatten the village if it was in the path of our advance and thought to be occupied by the enemy.

On one such occasion I distinctly remember seeing through my binoculars people running about, even though I was a good distance away. Moments later, our men launched their attack.

You had to be careful in the forward observation posts that your binoculars never hit a ray of sunlight, or your position would instantly be given away. Either you would have to move elsewhere, and waste the long, careful preparation involved in establishing the post, or you stayed put and risked being targeted by enemy artillery and shelled. The Germans were wonderful artillery men, nearly a match for our own. Their 88mm gun was anti-aircraft, anti-tank and land gun – a tremendous, triple-purpose killing machine. I can still hear it going off. Shrrrooom! Normally the noise of a big gun was much more drawn out – shhhrrrrrooooooooooom – but with that 88, it lasted no more than a split second. Then you would hear the 'crump, crump' of incoming mortar fire.

I may have hated the German soldiers, but I respected them, too. It wasn't their fault I had been dragged from my home and my carefree lifestyle in faraway Hawick to be fighting for my life in the mud and the rain of some Italian mountainside. There was only one man to be blamed for that: Adolf Hitler. The German troops were incredibly disciplined – maybe too disciplined, in the sense that their inflexibility undermined their ability to assess a situation on its own merits. A soldier would always think in terms of what his officer would say, and the officers almost always followed the textbook. The Germans were great ones for the manual, and nothing would divert them from it. The British soldiers, on the other hand, were more likely to play things by ear. They just dealt with whatever they saw unfolding before them according to the method they believed was most appropriate at that moment and in the prevailing circumstances. The Germans were not nearly as adaptable.

It was a precarious, difficult and stressful existence, and yet I would be giving totally the wrong impression if I implied that I hated every single waking moment of my war years. I didn't. Curiously enough, I loved Army life and I even enjoyed the action. I don't mind admitting that I was scared out of my wits half the time, but I did get a sense of satisfaction from it because I was proud to be serving my country. I was proud to be part of the big effort to clear the Germans out of Italy, and liked my job of lining up the enemy and calling for the guns to fire. It was an important role, and it made me feel I was really contributing to the war effort in a small but significant manner. The comradeship was special, too. Adversity forges strong bonds, and I felt I was helping others, and that in turn they were looking out for me.

And of course there was the odd lighter moment. One day I was put in charge of leading our regimental vehicles from one gun position to another. I was in the big armoured car at the front of the convoy with about forty-six vehicles behind me. I was able to follow the white tapes placed on the roads by our sappers to show us where all the mines had been laid and steer a safe course between them. But when we reached the town of Ravenna the white lines ran out. I was on my own, and my navigational skills were shaky at best. The entire convoy ended up going round Ravenna three times. After the second circuit, at least two guys in each of those forty-six trucks were standing up, gesticulating and shouting: 'Not bloody again! What's bloody goin' on?' I think that was the end of my days as a navigator.

Our 5th Medium Regiment supported the famous 2nd New Zealand Division, led by the legendary Lieutenant-General Sir Bernard Freyberg, through quite a bit of the Italian campaign. Although I'd been a home-bird as a youngster, these weren't the first New Zealanders I had come across. Back in Hawick in 1935, the All Blacks had arrived to play the South of Scotland in our town during their long tour of the British Isles. They were captained by a man named Jack Manchester, a towering figure in a dark brown scrum cap who led out his team for the game carrying the ball in one enormous hand. I can still remember the hushed awe that pervaded the ground as he walked on to the pitch. We local lads had never seen anything like it.

The New Zealand soldiers were tremendous fighters, the salt of the earth. Even the German Afrika Corps commander, Field-Marshal Erwin Rommel, thought them the best of all the opposing troops his men had faced. They were certainly the best of all the guys we supported in Italy. They had supreme confidence in their ability to get the job done, a trait that I think has been a feature of most All Black rugby teams through history. Perhaps it is a national characteristic. In any event, these New Zealanders displayed the same qualities as the All Black rugby men. They were committed, physically tough, dogged and refused to be beaten, attributes that have underpinned their rugby teams for a hundred years and more. They had tramline dedication to what had to be achieved. If the New Zealanders said they would take a certain hill by six o'clock in the morning, then by God, it would be taken. They were the kind of men you could always depend upon. And like the British they were flexible in their methods. They never bothered much with the textbook.

It is little wonder, then, that by this time, the Kiwis had also distinguished themselves in the desert. There is a marvellous, moving account of a New Zealand division written by Alan Moorehead in his outstanding trilogy dealing with the desert campaign. To me, it says everything about the New Zealand forces during the Second World War.

At last, we cut through a field of cactus and joined the main road north of Sousse. With the main road, we hit the New Zealand division coming head-on toward us – in the way the enemy would see it coming. They rolled by with their ranks and their guns and armoured cars, the finest troops of their kind in the world, the outflanking experts, the men who had fought the Germans in the desert for two years, the victors of half a dozen pitched battles. They were too gaunt and lean to be handsome, too hard and sinewy to be graceful, too youthful and physical to be complete. But if ever you wished to see the most resilient and practised fighter of the Anglo-Saxon armies, this was he. This wonderful division took a good deal of its fighting morale from its English General, Freyberg [Freyberg had been born in London], the VC who through two wars had probably been critically wounded more often than any other living man.

We were thrilled to bits when Lieutenant-General Freyberg himself came to a regimental dinner to thank us for our support. The great man, sporting his trademark cheesecutter cap, was introduced to all the officers that evening. He was out of the same mould as the All Black captain Jack Manchester – a big, broad man with grizzled features and a real aura about him.

'And where do you come from?' he asked me when it was my turn to be presented to him.

When he looked at you, his strong, clear eyes seemed to pierce right through to your inner soul and you had the feeling that in that momentary appraisal he was seeing a good deal about you. I was mightily impressed. He was friendly, but there was an element of grim resolve to him, too.

'From Hawick, in the south of Scotland, sir,' I replied.

'Oh, they play rugby there, don't they?'

I smiled and confirmed that yes, they did. But so much had happened that it seemed a long, long time since I had been in Hawick playing rugby.

Lieutenant-General Freyberg made a point of saying that our artillery had done especially well at Monte Cassino. Our targets had tended to be little sections of mountain along the bottom of the big hill on which the monastery was perched, and it hadn't been easy striking the right one. But we had managed it more times than not, and we took a lot of pride in our accuracy and in that tribute.

My job, directing our gunners to the targets, was one thing; crawling up a mountainside battlefield, gaining about fifteen yards of ground in an hour, and under constant attack, was sheer hell for the infantry boys. The Germans, sitting on the summit, popping out from little peepholes, held all the advantages, and at times our progress slowed to only a yard or two at a time.

When the Germans shelled your gun position, you built yourself into a slit trench and stayed there until it stopped, because they were extremely accurate with those 88mm guns. You could hear the shrapnel whizzing through the air. It became a bit of a joke in our regiment that you'd never see me standing up when the guns were going off. A soldier once asked me why I always got into the slit trench first and I replied, 'Because I'm an officer and you're a gunner.'

Although a lot of the time I was terrified, I wouldn't say I ever got to the point of total despair. But not everyone could handle it. One day I came across a British soldier who had simply cracked up under the pressure. I was investigating a farmhouse which had just been shelled. Its roof had been blown off, and I was thinking of setting up an observation post there. Inside I discovered this guy sitting, or rather lying, in the corner, his knees tucked right up under his chin in an almost foetal position. Finding him there gave me quite a shock. He was shaking violently and had a disturbing, wild-eyed look about him. Talking to him had no effect whatsoever: he just carried on staring at the wall. Clearly he was shell-shocked. I felt so sorry for him – he'd obviously had a terrible experience of some kind. I arranged for him to be taken back to the 'wagon lines', as we called the rear echelon. A Moroccan medical battalion were among those who helped care for the wounded and sick. It was the task of others to scour the battlefield after an engagement, collecting up the bodies and shattered limbs that had been left behind.

As an officer, I was always aware of the fact that you were expected to set standards for the other ranks to follow. It was made clear to you that officers had to behave differently. Your men followed your orders because they had faith in your ability and leadership, and you had to retain that trust. So in battle, when shells were landing among you and your men, you had to show you could cope with the pressure and not panic. I don't mind saying that I was very proud to be an officer. It was a big responsibility, but I liked it.

The battle for Cassino seemed to last for ever. At one point it felt like we had been out there for about fifteen years and would likely be there another fifteen. It was a terrible place. The pounding of the monastery went on day and night. One German soldier wrote in his diary: 'We are back in the hills behind Cassino. What we are going through here is beyond description. I never experienced anything like this in Russia, not even a second's peace only the dreadful thunder of guns and mortars and there are the planes over and above. Everything is in the hands of fate, and many of the boys have met theirs already.' So, too, had many of our boys. In the end, even the Germans could not hold out. We finally scaled the last of the peaks and opened up the road to Rome, the north and the entire peninsula. But the gateway had been breached at huge cost. By the time it was all over, 250,000 men had been either killed or wounded.

Once we had overrun the German positions, we carried on up through Italy, past Rimini and then across and up beyond Genoa. Shooting, shelling, killing day and night, became a routine. We were almost hedge-hopping. All the way, the New Zealanders continued to do a terrific job, driving forward relentlessly, again and again, even though they were losing many men, most through incredible acts of personal bravery. The Germans were bloody good soldiers but not even they could withstand the Kiwis with us in support.

Also active in this theatre of the European war were several Indian and Gurkha divisions, all wonderfully courageous in combat. Like the New Zealanders, their troops must have wondered at times what the hell they were doing so far from home in a war that seemed to have no relevance to their own lives. There were also the Poles. The 2nd Carpathian Division were renowned fighters but once they got behind a steering wheel they became absolutely fearless dirt-track riders. Whenever there was a Polish regiment on the road, everybody else got off! But they were amazingly brave and staunch allies.

And then, of course, there were the Americans, who had officially come into the war back in December 1941 when the Japanese had attacked Pearl Harbor. From that point on, the vast industrial strength of the USA had bolstered the Allied war effort immensely, and enormous loads of arms and armour made their way across the perilous waters of the North Atlantic Ocean to help the fight for Europe. When the invasion came, first in north Africa and then in Europe, Americans were there in massive numbers. They were heavily involved in the Italian campaign, too, where the American General Mark Clark was the Allied Commander.

I got a big surprise one day, crouching in my forward observation post, watching for signs of German positions through the binoculars. I heard a jeep coming up the track behind me, which was not uncommon. The path was protected from enemy view by the steep rise of the land, and sometimes an officer would come up to discuss tactics and progress.

But imagine my astonishment when the jeep stopped and out climbed General Mark Clark. I snapped to attention. He returned the salute, and smiled.

'How is it going?' he asked, addressing me as 'Lieutenant'.

'Not bad, sir,' I replied. 'We're trying to get fire down on that position over that peak.'

Clark took my binoculars and had a look for himself to get a view of the situation from the forward post. We chatted for a few minutes and he asked me if I needed anything up there. I told him I was happy I could do the job and he seemed satisfied. It was just a friendly conversation, really. I remember studying him, just as I had Lieutenant-General Freyberg, but I don't recall much about him other than that he had quite a big nose. I certainly didn't get a sense of anything like the aura the New Zealand division's leader had about him. All the same, he was the big chief, the man running the whole show, and here he was, up in the hills, talking to me. We always felt that we, the ordinary soldiers, bore the brunt of the privations and horrors of the war, so to see General Mark Clark on some godforsaken mountainside impressed us all. For it was dangerous, of course. Positions like that were often shelled. It made you feel that the senior officers had not forgotten you; that they were interested in what you were doing, and in seeing the war from your vantage point. Some may cynically regard that sort of appearance as a mere morale-boosting exercise, but to me Clark's hands-on approach underlined the combined resolve of the Allies to get the war won.

There were some rumblings of disquiet and discontent when the Americans brazenly paraded into Rome, basking in the glory of liberating the Eternal City. While some of us were trekking up steep mountainsides in rough terrain, being shot at by the retreating German troops, they were sweeping northwards along the flatter coastal plain, easier country to negotiate. Doubtless it was a battle plan decided by those on high, but we always felt that our regiment, and the British in general, were handed the short straw. In fairness, though, the Americans were a tremendous force. They didn't have the reputation of being the most accurate of artillery men, but they were brave and wholehearted – there were no half-measures with them.

When it was all over, I didn't have a lot of sympathy for the Germans. They had followed a maniac and lost everything. In the Army, you have to look after yourself and concern yourself only with your pals, your regiment and your job. Everybody had a role, and one of the great things about the British Army, and especially the guys I came across, was that they all had a clear idea of what theirs was. You felt that people were interested in you and concerned for your welfare. Although I was an officer of comparatively modest rank, I never felt remote from those higher up.

When I eventually got home, I knew that I was a different person. The boy I'd been was gone. I suspect he disappeared for ever on that awful morning in that village cemetery somewhere in Italy. I'd never seen anything like what I saw there and, I'm glad to say, I've never seen anything like it since. I never want to, either. We had left to go to war feeling a mixture of pride and fear. We had no idea what to expect, what was going to happen to us, and no control over our own destiny. You had to go where others told you and do exactly as they said. We all simply had to follow the orders of our superiors. Such as one famous in the regiment, our colonel, 'Crusher' Hayes, a man with a bristling moustache, the physique of a prop forward and a lovely upper-class accent. The epitome of the British Army officer – a thoroughly good chap. Crusher had already moved his men into a field when he was informed it was mined. Undeterred, he took his soldiers through the field regardless, leading the way himself. That was Crusher. He took chances but his creed was clear. 'We will show them, chaps,' was his catch-phrase. We all had a soft spot for Crusher.

But such experiences do bring maturity and self-assurance. Certainly, I personally felt I was a more rounded individual for having spent those years at war. I had seen the good and bad in human beings. It was a rough and brutal introduction to what life can be, but perhaps a valuable one, nonetheless. It also gave me a greater appreciation of the home and life I was fortunate enough to have.

Many years after the war had ended, I went back to Italy for a holiday at Rimini. It was summertime, and you could not walk on the sand, it was so baking hot. It brought back vivid memories of the intense, boiling heat, the flies, the dust and the calls of the dying. Much more recently, when Scotland were playing Italy in Rome in the 2002 Six Nations Championship, I returned to the valley above which a rebuilt Monte Cassino now stands. With me were my wife Bette, daughter Linda and son-in-law Alan. Being there again and looking up at Monte Cassino on the very summit of the mountain was an eerie feeling. I thought of all the terrible times I had endured there and reflected, too, on the brave British soldiers who had gone there with me but never came back. It is an awe-inspiring place. It is hard enough to believe that people could build such a creation on a mountain peak, still less that an army could chase off its occupants. It looks today, since being rebuilt, as it did in 1944, impregnable. In the surrounding countryside there were cemeteries everywhere, filled with little white crosses commemorating soldiers from countries all over the world. That was the gruesome reality of war. What a waste it was of fine young men.

I didn't give a thought to rugby football in those days. The war put everything else into perspective. But at the end of the hostilities, when I got a game for the Combined Services in Italy, I was chuffed to bits. It was such a relief from the tension and anxiety of military action. To get out on a rugby pitch and hoof the ball about in complete freedom was just magical. It's strange how it is the simplest pleasures that often mean the most to us.

In May 1945, there was one more special job to

confront when I was ordered to take charge of a jail in Milan. Most young boys dream about what they would like to do for a living when they grow up, a wish list that can encompass everything from train or bus driver, through lawyer, doctor or politician, to sports commentator, footballer or astronaut. But I doubt that prison governor features on many of them. It had certainly never been on mine, and it was not an appealing prospect now.

It was just my bad luck to be in the wrong place at the wrong time. Milan, to be precise, where my regiment was billeted at the end of the war. On the face of it, it wasn't a bad place to be. The whole of Europe was in chaos, but at least Milan hadn't been bombed to bits as so many other European cities had. Our artillery and the generals had a deep respect for the historic parts of Italy, and Milan, like Rome and the Vatican, had escaped comparatively lightly. On a pleasant, sunny day it was a lovely city. I played rugby there for the brigade team and wherever we went, whether it was as a regiment or as individuals, we were welcomed with open arms by the local people. Sometimes we were handed free drinks and occasionally some food, although most of the time we had to make do with our own rations, almost always the wretched bully beef, a delicacy of which I had long since become heartily sick. There was little we could do to introduce any variety. I do remember one occasion when about ten of our gunners pooled their allowance and poured the lot – tins of spam, macaroni, bully beef – into one huge pan, setting it over a fire of sticks. When the feast was cooked, they fell on it like wolves on their prey, gobbling it all up as if they hadn't seen food for months. I took one look at this ghastly offering and immediately lost my appetite.

The Italian people seemed to have respect for the British Army. They were afraid of the Germans, ostensibly their allies, but their attitude to us was one of regard rather than fear. At heart, the Italians are very decent people. I doubt whether many of them ever wanted to become embroiled in a bloody war in the first place, but Benito Mussolini, their leader, had thought otherwise. Worse still, he had chosen the wrong side to join.

In spite of the air of relative normality in Milan, the chaotic aftermath of war lurked beneath the surface and there were plenty of rogue individuals roaming around the place. In the city's guardroom, of which I was to take charge, we came across some serious villains – Nazis and Italian criminals awaiting trial for armed robbery and murder – among the deserting Allied soldiers and other assorted people who needed to be locked up for one reason or another. The guardroom had been converted from a reformatory, which had previously housed more youthful inmates. There were bars and wire around the outside, and the front gates were strong, solid metal cemented into tall brick pillars on either side. I had expected more of a run-down establishment but, truth to tell, it was surprisingly smart for a prison. I say prison, but it was more of a detention centre, really, and that was what made our lives so difficult, because it was a hell of a lot easier to get out of than a proper jail. All the same it was pretty grim. It intimidated me, so what effect it had on some of the less hardened prisoners, heaven only knows.

Then there was an English fellow called Guy Fleming who had absconded from his unit and set up home locally with an Italian woman. A slightly built chap, he had made a fortune out of stealing British Army surplus stuff and selling it to the Italians. As someone said, perhaps he should have been given a medal. The authorities found out that he had been involved with some Italian brigands and that he had bank accounts all over the place. Some people go to war to fight; others to rob and pilfer for their own benefit. Another Englishman, called Ruff, had, it turned out, spent most of his life in prison and was totally ruthless. He was hell-bent on escaping from wherever he was incarcerated, and I was worried about him and Fleming: they were both callous and tenacious, just the types to hatch an escape plan. I told the 'warders', who were part of the untrained support staff I had been given, to watch these two like hawks. If they broke out, yours truly would be on the carpet having to explain how I'd let them get away. Luckily, however, even though none of us guarding these guys had any experience whatsoever of prisons or how they operated, we managed to keep security tight enough to hold them.

But the threat of breakout was never far from my mind. At night I would lie awake worrying incessantly about it. Of course, it was ludicrous to have put me in charge in the first place – I was an artillery man, not a jailer. Nevertheless I knew it would be a black mark against my name if anyone did get away. As it happened, two men who were deemed lower-risk prisoners did escape briefly one day, but with the help of another inmate we got them back. I had given this fellow a job in the kitchen, what you might call something of a cushy number, and he repaid my faith in him by coming to me after the birds had flown and telling me where they were going. The Military Police went to their hiding-place and caught them like rats in a trap. So in the end it was a very satisfactory day's business for us.

On another occasion an Italian charged with ill-treating British prisoners-of-war was brought in. Word spreads around any jail like a virus, and soon everybody knew what this man was accused of. He should have been completely segregated when he was taken for his morning exercise in the yard (every prisoner was allowed eighty minutes' exercise each day) but alas, a couple of other men had not vacated the exercise area with the others. One of them, a guy of oriental descent, a huge specimen, got hold of this Italian and gave him a hell of a beating. The Italian was brought in to see me in my office and I don't know who winced the most, him from his injuries or me out of concern for what my superiors might have to say about the incident. He was due to appear in court twenty-four hours later and it was going to look marvellous, this prisoner being led in bloodied and bruised and sporting a couple of whopping black eyes from another inmate's fists. We had to get the MO out to patch him up as best he could before we sent the man off to court.

I was in charge of that jail for three weeks. It seemed more like three years. The responsibility and my awareness of how ill-equipped I was to take it on was frightening. But finally, I was relieved to be, well, relieved, and returned to the regiment for the remainder of my active service. It was just normal duties, making sure the guns were kept clean and going through various drills so that we could produce them under pressure. I loved all that.

After the fighting had stopped, many people took the opportunity to re-evaluate their lives and what they wanted to do with them. I very nearly took a career direction that would have meant never becoming a rugby commentator. Staying in the forces was definitely an option and I was encouraged to think about it by a couple of senior officers, including our second-in-command, Lieutenant-Colonel Pearce, who outlined the advantages of signing on as an officer in the regular Army. I came very, very close to putting pen to paper committing myself to a twenty-one-year term of duty. You see, I'd enjoyed the comradeship so much that I was concerned that I might feel lonely and insecure away from the Army. Making a career of it represented the continuation of the wonderful togetherness I had enjoyed so much, despite all the privations.

But at the last minute, almost literally as the pen hovered above the form, I changed my mind. It was the thought of Hawick that stopped me. I had missed my home very much while I was in Italy, and it was likely that if I went somewhere else I'd feel the same. If that were so, it seemed a strange career choice to go into something that would take me away so often, and for long periods. Indeed, had I signed, I'd probably have been stuck somewhere like Egypt for twenty years or so. Unquestionably I would have ended up fighting the Chinese in Korea in 1948. I think I could have done without that.

So, having negotiated German snipers and artillery gunners, the worst excesses of the Italian climate and the physical fatigue and mental traumas associated with war, not to mention the dreadful Milan guardhouse, Temporary Captain William Pollock McLaren was at last demobbed in February 1947. I didn't expect to be received as a conquering hero when I eventually got home to Hawick, and I wasn't. There were plenty of us. I was just glad to be back with my loved ones again and to meet up with my friends, most of whom I hadn't seen for four or five years. But of course, my homecoming was tinged with sadness when it quickly emerged that a lot of them had not come back from their own theatres of war, and never would. Like me, they had accepted the risks in Europe and just got on with it. I had been one of the lucky ones. I survived.

So it was one of life's ironies that, having cheated death on the battlefields of Italy, I should find it once again lurking round the corner back in the comfort and safety of Hawick.

CHAPTER 4
TUBERCULOSIS

I AM EIGHTY YEARS OLD NOW, A MAN WHO HAS BEEN fortunate to live a long life. But there was a time when I thought I would not see my twenty-fifth birthday.

By Christmas 1947, I had at last begun to leave the war behind me. I was enrolled on a physical education course at Woolmanhill College, Aberdeen, in preparation for a career in teaching. I was a busy young man, studying hard, training every day, socialising and playing as much rugby as possible. That March – almost as soon as I had got back from Italy – I had met Bette, the girl who was to become my wife, at a dance at Hawick Town Hall. I had been captivated by her beauty and charm and we agreed to see each other again. From then on we met regularly whenever I was home from college.

Life was taking shape once again, though it was

still tough in its own way. Rationing remained in force – indeed, food rationing would continue in Britain until the early 1950s – which meant sweets, cheese, meat and fruit were in desperately short supply, other than on the black market. Luckily, Bette had an uncle who was the manager of a fish shop and also worked for the Co-op, and he was able to point us in the right direction to get black-market supplies.

Before the year was out, I received a call-up from the Scottish selectors for a national trial match at Murrayfield. I was overjoyed. The road to a much-coveted Scottish cap lay within tantalising reach. I'd regained my fitness after the war, playing a bit of rugby in Italy and returning in earnest to the game as soon as the 1947–8 season began. I was doing a lot of physical training work up at Aberdeen that was putting me in excellent shape and I thought I was in the prime of health. Yet I had a suspicion that something was not quite right.

When I'd been out with Bette I used to take her back to her house in Fisher Avenue, on the other side of the town from where I lived, and say goodnight on her front doorstep. Few people had cars in those days and the buses didn't run that late, so I used to run home, through the cold, the dark and, all too often, the rain. I regarded it as just another part of my fitness programme.

Looking back later, I realised that the alarm bells should have sounded during those runs, because I'd begun to struggle to make them, and I couldn't understand why. I felt a bit of a pain in my chest and I didn't seem to have as much energy as usual. One night I was puffing so hard I had to stop and get my breath back. Needing to do that on a mile-long run should have been a warning to me, but when you are young, you don't worry about these things. You think you are invincible.

Catching sight of myself in a mirror, I started to notice a figure that was thinner, more haggard and drawn. I had probably been overdoing it, I told myself. After all, at college we were up and out running by seven in the morning, and then we'd go swimming. In both summer and winter we would go on until eight, nine or ten at night with classes. A three-year course was being squeezed into just fourteen months, which put an immense physical pressure on everyone involved. Clearly I was rundown; apart from that, there wasn't anything to worry about. I'd survived a war, started training for a new career and I was playing rugby again. What could possibly be wrong with me? However, I did take the precaution of going to see my local doctor and explaining I felt a bit below par. He told me what I'd suspected myself: I had simply been working too hard. Best to ease up a bit for a while. It seemed sensible advice.

I did play in one Scotland trial match. I was unfortunate because I was placed opposite W.I.D. Elliot, who was recognised as one of the best Scottish forwards of all time. He was a Borders farmer and a great back-row player, a real handful. He was so powerful and strong they threw a lot of line-out balls to him at the back. I was replaced at the interval by another fellow they wanted to have a look at. I was sad not to win a cap: just one cap would have done me fine. But when I look back, just to be in the Murrayfield dressing room – hallowed ground for me – among all those star players was an extraordinary experience.

I continued with my course, but I was disturbed to find myself growing weaker and weaker. I was losing weight – altogether it amounted to around two stone. I had just about managed to complete my course when I returned to my doctor for another check-up. This time I was worried, and justifiably so, as it turned out. The diagnosis, once tests had been carried out, was alarming. I had tuberculosis. The doctor's words whizzed at me like German machine-gun bullets back on the slopes of that Italian mountain four years earlier. I had taken too much out of myself, I was told. When I remembered the long runs I had done through the cold, rain and even snow up in Aberdeen, I found it hard to argue with that explanation.

I was stunned, upset and very frightened. How could I have come through all those long months of fighting only to contract this awful disease? For as everyone knew, tuberculosis was a killer, and there was no cure. One day I was playing for Hawick down at Mansfield Park against Kelso, and within a couple of weeks I was in hospital. It was hard to find anything positive to focus on, for I knew that even if I could somehow survive the illness, a long spell in hospital was inevitable. Everything had seemed to be going my way. I was on the brink of a fine career and possibly a Scotland cap, something I longed to achieve. What would happen to all that now? What about my relationship with the girl of whom I was already so fond, and who I knew, deep down, I loved and wanted to marry? I could hardly expect her to hang around a sick person, perhaps for years, just because we'd got on so well since a dance at the Town Hall. And that was looking on the bright side. In truth, the chances were that I would die.

I was admitted to Bangour Hospital for six months, and then moved to East Fortune Sanatorium, south of Edinburgh, which had been a wartime aerodrome. I was attended by doctors W.A. Murray and R.W. Biagi, who diagnosed TB, as tuberculosis was widely known, in the left lung. Because it was in the lung rather than the spine, which was where some people contracted it, you coughed an awful lot and produced a great deal of phlegm. I will never forget those awful, rasping coughs that racked my now frail body. It felt as if all my innards were trying to come up. All the time, you were producing blood in the spittle. You had to spit it into a receptacle that was taken away for analysis.

Lying there in bed and taking in the surroundings was one of the most utterly depressing things I have ever had to face in my entire life. There were rows and rows of beds in that ward, all filled with people suffering from this deadly disease, many of them young men and women in the prime of life. When you walked down the corridor, all you could hear was this terrible wheezing and so many people coughing. Although I'm by no means a regular churchgoer, I have always had a bit of a religious side

– my mother was religious and could quote from the Bible quite extensively. I certainly started to pray pretty hard then.

The doctors and nurses were under huge strain due to the sheer numbers of patients. TB had swept across much of Europe and the epidemic was later attributed to the poor health of so many people during and after the war. Bad living conditions and diet were very important factors, so families who were hard up and couldn't afford to eat properly were very prone to catching it. So, too, were ex-soldiers, worn down by the years of deprivation and suffering. Doctors later told me that I almost certainly first contracted the disease in Milan, working at the guardroom. That damned place. But where you caught it was pretty irrelevant, as it was spreading at such an alarming rate that it was becoming almost a plague of modern times. To see so many fine young people brought to their sickbeds by this illness, lying there apparently just waiting to die, was terrible. You wouldn't have wished it on your worst enemy.

As soon as I was transferred to East Fortune, the doctors told me how serious my illness was. They said I could expect to be in there for as long as four years – provided I could stay alive that long.

Four years! It was like a prison sentence. The news hit me like a fist in the face.

I tried in vain to come to terms with what had happened to me. There was no crumb of comfort to be had, it seemed. The best the doctors could offer was the hope that a new medical solution, which researchers all over the world were desperately seeking, would be found. The environment was hardly conducive to keeping your spirits up, either. The sanatorium was shabby. The paint on the corridor walls was peeling; the fittings old, many of them decrepit. The war had stretched the economy of the country and the government had little spare cash for anything, least of all refinements for hospitals up on the remote east coast of Scotland. Worse, patients were dying around you almost every day. The first clue that something serious was going on was the urgent pulling of the plastic screens around a bed in a ward. Just one look at the expression on the faces of the doctors re-emerging from behind the screens told you whether someone else had succumbed.

The spore-producing TB bacteria thrived in the saliva and mucus in the mouth. When an infected person sneezed or coughed, those bacteria were released into the air and so, in theory, anyone could catch the disease by inhalation. That was why the lungs were the most common site of infection. Once inhaled, the bacteria ate away the lung tissue, creating a cavity. In the advanced stages of infection, the bacteria destroyed the blood vessels of the lungs, causing the patient to cough up blood. Some of the nurses wore white surgical masks to protect themselves, although the doctors did not seem to, even though the disease was highly contagious. Perhaps that was a good thing for the patients, at least: a masked doctor looming over them with a large needle might have made them even more terrified than they already were.

For the first year or so, I spent almost all day and all night in bed, submitting myself to whatever form of medical intervention the doctors decided I needed. As there was no known cure for TB, this was inevitably something of a hit-and-hope effort. Complete rest was considered essential, to give any treatment the best chance of success. In my case this consisted mainly of pneumoperitoneum treatment, which involved having a needle about five inches long stuck into the right side of my abdomen to pump air under the diaphragm and lift the lung. The aim was to get the lung into a position where it could rest, giving it as much help as possible to repair itself.

The first time I saw Dr Biagi coming to my bedside

with his huge great needle I asked nervously: 'What are you going to do with *that*?'

'I'm going to put it in your abdomen,' he replied.

'Get away. You can't do that.'

'I'm afraid I shall have to.'

And he did – every Friday for what turned out to be almost two years. Enduring this weekly drilling was tough. No wonder I still don't like Fridays. The injection was frightening and left you with the strangest feeling, as if you were somehow all puffed up.

In addition to the pneumoperitoneum treatment there were injections of calcium chlorate to try to close the cavity the TB had created in the lung, and something called the phrenic crush, whereby the phrenic nerve, close to the collarbone, was literally crushed so that it would compress and immobilise the affected lung, helping to lift it up and rest it. I was fortunate that only one of my lungs was damaged: sometimes patients who had cavities in both lungs, or whose hearts were infected, could not stand the trauma of that particular procedure.

Otherwise, all you could do was rest over a long period, ideally, it was believed, in a dry climate. Clear, fresh mountain air was considered the perfect environment, but that option was not available to us in our part of Scotland. I've always enjoyed fresh air, but I must say I had never envisaged taking it the way we did at East Fortune – spending the nights outdoors in our beds. Whatever the weather, we were wheeled outside on to the veranda, wrapped warmly in rugs but with our heads sticking out so that we could breathe in the healing air. The fact that it might be snowing didn't seem to bother the doctors at all. The nurses simply put waterproof covers over our bedding and left us to get on with it. It was a novel experience.

Also considered essential was a diet rich in fat and therefore calories. The theory was that the best combination to fight TB was a mixture of honey, hot milk, butter and lard. It was said to be thoroughly good for you – if you could keep that lot down.

I came closer to despair during that time than at any other stage of my life, before or since. Even in the war, when the Germans were hurling shells at us and those awful Nebelwerfer guns (six-barrelled mortars known as 'moaning minnies' to the troops) were making their terrible whining noise as they flew off the rocket launch-pad in our direction, it was possible to keep up your morale. You knew you were fighting for good against evil, you had your chums around you and there was that sense that you were all in it together, and no one would let anyone else down. But this . . . this was completely different.

The saddest thing was constantly seeing your fellow patients, especially those you had got friendly with and chatted to every day, suddenly decline and then die. The rate at which they seemed to go downhill was truly frightening. We all lived with death, day and night. There were sixteen to twenty patients on my ward. One of them was a former miner from Fife, a big, burly, hearty guy called Stewart, whose brother played soccer for East Fife FC. Stewart was a gem of a fellow. He cheered everyone up. When he was well enough to be able to get up and walk around – an 'up-patient' as the hospital called them – he brought the rest of us cups of tea and chortled away the hours with us. I had such a regard for that guy. He had had TB of the spine, and if you got that, you were in for a very long recovery period, if indeed you survived at all. They reckoned on eighteen months before you even started to get better, and some of these patients had been in East Fortune for four or five years.

I couldn't help feeling pessimistic and my family didn't find it easy to cheer me up. They were wonderful, all the same. My father and other members of my family all came to see me and tried very hard to lift my mood. Bette came, too – so marvellously regularly that I was quickly confirmed in my knowledge that she was indeed the one for me. Sadly, I had no expectation of ever getting out of that place . . . or being able to marry her. When they left after a visit, I would quietly pull the sheets over my head, snuggle myself down into the bed and cry my eyes out. Great dollops of tears would cascade down my cheeks on to the sheet. I felt bereft of hope and, increasingly, of life. I felt a dreadful emptiness and loneliness, combined with a fear that never went away. I was well aware of just how ill I was, and there was no escaping the inevitable conclusion. It was only going to be a matter of time before I died.

I was scared stiff and feared that very soon it would be my body they would be wheeling away under a sheet. Motivating yourself in those circumstances was enormously difficult.

It had become increasingly clear to me that Bette felt much the same way about me as I did about her. The fact that she was there at all ought to have signalled that as clearly as flags on the mast of a ship. She came every weekend, catching the train from Hawick, fifty-five miles away in the Borders, all the way up to Edinburgh. There she would board the bus that left the eastern side of the city for a half-hour journey down the coast to East Fortune. The bus was full of relatives of sanatorium patients, and Bette said that many a time the return trip to Edinburgh was made to the accompaniment of sobs from some of the passengers who had arrived to find that their loved ones had just passed away. Trying to keep up your own spirits in those circumstances, never mind anyone else's, was a mountainous task. Yet, heroically, she made that journey every week for nineteen months, slogging through all weathers.

Often she brought me in food which she had made herself or been given by family and friends. Among them was R.T. Smith, our local baker, a great bull of a man who had played rugby for Kelso and Scotland. He would stand at the door of his shop waiting for Bette to come along on her way to the station and hand her a nice big fruit cake. It was a lovely gesture, because I didn't actually know him. Many of the townsfolk seemed aware of my illness and where I was, and were full of sympathy and practical assistance. Hawick is a small community and if you are in any sort of trouble, people will help. There is a real kinship among the local people; they are truly special. Other friends gave Bette food coupons. It was much appreciated, as the food in the hospital, usually steamed fish, was unappetising. Not that any of the patients was well enough even to fancy the idea of a five-course meal, obviously, but something different or home-cooked was more of a temptation to the palate than the standard fare.

On Saturdays, after her visit, Bette would stay in Edinburgh for the night with a friend, Mrs Allirina Webster, who was very kind to her. On the Sunday, she would be back at East Fortune. Sunday afternoons, just after she had gone, were the worst times for me. I knew I wouldn't see her for a whole week, and I also knew what I had to face every day in the meantime.

My fears about the likely outcome of my illness troubled me constantly, and in the end I decided I had to be cruel to be kind. I made up my mind to tell Bette that she was wasting her time, that she shouldn't be coming every weekend to see me because I was not likely to survive the weeks and months to come. So when she arrived the following Saturday, bearing another parcel of food, I did not open it up at once, as I usually did. Instead I looked at her as firmly in the eye as I could without bursting into tears, and said simply: 'You cannot go on like this. You must find yourself someone else who is fit and healthy. You can't carry on hanging around waiting for someone as sick as I am.' I just about got the words out, but it was hard, I can tell you.

Bette just smiled sweetly, apparently oblivious of what I was trying to tell her. 'Well, don't you be worrying yourself about that,' she replied. 'We are going to see this thing through together, and you will get better – I know you will. Then we can talk about whether we want to carry on seeing one another.'

That took the wind right out of my sails. But at least I had told her what I felt, and my conscience was clear. It was up to Bette from then on. As it was, her continuing kindness, love for and devotion to me, and my own feelings for her, prompted us not to part but, not that long afterwards, to do the exact opposite. On one of her weekend visits I got the nurses to pull the curtains round my bed for some privacy and asked Bette if she would marry me. There came one of those golden smiles that have lit up her face so often during our many years together, and she said, 'Yes, of course.' It was a special moment and one that, at last, was able to lift me. She, more than anyone, helped me fight on. Her love was giving me a reason to live and I am sure now that without her I would have gone under.

However, having a purpose in life could not, of course, alter my physical state. There was absolutely nothing you could do about TB other than hope that the treatment worked eventually. The doctors came to see me for a chat one day. There was no real change in my condition, they said; hardly encouraging news, but then, I had not expected anything different. However, a new drug had recently been introduced and they wondered whether I would be prepared to try it. I was left in little doubt that I would be pretty much a guinea pig for this drug, and that there were no guarantees whatsoever as to what it might achieve. I agreed. I didn't see that I had a great deal to lose. I wasn't likely to survive anyway, so I might as well try anything that gave me half a chance.

The new drug was called streptomycin, and it had literally only just been discovered. I started taking it, and a couple of weeks later I was summoned to the doctors' consulting rooms. Imagine my astonishment – not to mention theirs – when the doctors compared two X-rays. One was of my damaged lung when I had first been admitted, the other was of the same lung a week before, after a short time on this new course of treatment. The evidence was unmistakable: the cavity in the lung was beginning to close.

It was hard to say who was more shocked by this news, the doctors or me. I can remember them just staring and staring at these X-rays, as though there must be something wrong somewhere. 'We can't believe this improvement,' one of them said. But the proof was there, right in front of our eyes. It seemed, suddenly, as though a miracle had occurred. I was taken back to my bed, this emaciated figure, two stones lighter than I had been at the start and hollow-cheeked, and shed a few more tears, not out of fear of dying this time, but relief. At last I had cause for hope that I might now somehow beat this terrible disease.

Of course, I was by no means out of the woods yet. But I continued with the streptomycin – and I continued to recover. Slowly but surely, I began to feel a little better, a little stronger each day. I was not coughing as much now, and when I did there were fewer occasions when it produced blood. Then I graduated to becoming an up-patient. I was allowed to get up for about two hours in the afternoons, to start with, and go for a little walk. It was like being released from a prison cell. After a while that was increased to four hours a day. Finally the time came when I could be up all day, helping to take cups of tea to frailer patients, just as big Stewart and others had done for me.

As a fully fledged up-patient, I began to feel sufficiently strong to start involving myself in some of the activities on offer at the sanatorium to keep the patients occupied. There was an *East Fortune* magazine, and I wrote some articles for that and generally assisted with putting it together. Then I helped cut out the holes for a putting green on the lawn outside our ward and arranged putting competitions. There were table-tennis contests, too. At last some fun began to seep back into my life. It was vital therapy for all of us, for time had hung heavily while we'd been lying in bed for a year or more.

Then there were the craft skills. You thought I was only ever a rugby player and commentator? You were wrong. In that isolation hospital, yours truly worked so hard making rugs that my fingers bled. I had this long needle (probably one of those they'd plunged into my abdomen so often it had become blunt) threaded with wool which, day after day, I would yank through the tough backing of the rug's base, positioning it neatly in rows. Sometimes I would manage only one row in a whole day before I was tired out, and it took me months to make one rug. But by the time I left the hospital, I had produced four or five. I made leather handbags and photo frames, too, and I still have one of each – and one of those rugs – upstairs in my home today, forty-five years later.

Finally, there came the day when the doctors were able to confirm the miracle for certain. The revolutionary new treatment had saved my life. Before long, it also enabled me to walk out of the East Fortune Sanatorium at last, after nineteen months there. I went home to Hawick scarcely daring to believe I had survived.

It had been the worst time of my life, and yet strangely, it was perhaps the best in that it gave me the greatest perspective on our existence that a young man could possibly have. I had spent the best part of seven years hovering between life and death. Almost immediately after the horrors of Italy this life-threatening illness had forced me to fight for my life again, but this time it had been a personal battle against a sustained attack by an enemy far more tenacious than the Germans. I had confronted death head-on, and somehow lived to tell the tale.

Before I went to war, rugby football had never been far from my thoughts, day or night. By the time I walked out of East Fortune Sanatorium, winning or losing a rugby match did not seem terribly important to me any more. Now simple pleasures gave me greater joy than almost anything else. What had emerged was a different man, a wiser man, for sure, but above all one who was just happy to smell the grass in summer and sweep up the leaves in autumn; to appreciate and enjoy the fundamental everyday things that are the foundation of our lives.

Most importantly, in Bette I had found true love in someone who would remain my closest friend for the rest of my days.

CHAPTER 5
CHILDHOOD

IN THE HOURS WHEN THE DAYLIGHT WAS FADING, AS I lay on my bed in the TB isolation hospital in that state between consciousness and semi-consciousness, in my mind I was far, far away from those grim surroundings. I was a young boy once again.

It was Christmas morning, 1931, and I was bounding down the stairs of our three-bedroomed council house at 57 Weensland Road, Hawick. My mother and father were smiling broadly as I walked across the room to them and they handed me a present. It felt soft, a strange shape, too. I tore off the wrapping paper, as all young children do, in a state of high excitement and anticipation.

There it sat in my hands. A new leather rugby ball, one of those old ones with the laces down the front. I could not have been more thrilled. I rushed straight out of the house, ignoring my mother's calls to put on some warm clothes, and headed for the patch of common land in front of the house where the youngsters of Weensland Road went for their kick-abouts, to practise my goal-kicking.

In my imagination I was standing on the pitch at Murrayfield. The crowd was hushed. I glanced down at the Scottish thistle on my left breast, proudly displayed against the dark blue of the national jersey. I checked my stance, my posture, too. Then I approached the ball and gave it a right good thump. It sailed, straight and true, through the goalposts at Murrayfield. The crowd were on their feet, cheering: Scotland were on their way to another victory over the auld enemy, England, and I was the hero of the hour.

That bit of land on the estate was pretty sizeable and we local kids held rugby internationals on it most days. Conveniently, there was a pair of lamp-posts at each end – two natural sets of goalposts, and floodlit rugby into the bargain! The pitch itself left a little to be desired, though. The ground was too hard and uneven for proper tackling so if you got touched, you had to pass. Even when my pals weren't around for a game, I would be out there at some point every day, hoofing the ball and disturbing everyone at all hours. I was quite happy practising my kicking by myself. A friend and neighbour, Joe Hunter, who was a great golfing buddy of Dad's, lived in a house that overlooked the pitch, and he used to come out and stand at his front door, saying, 'Use your other foot, Billy!' 'Uncle Joe', as much as anybody, encouraged me to learn to kick with both left and right and in the end I became quite good at it. The ability to drop a goal with either foot proved very useful in my early days as a centre threequarter or stand-off half.

There were some great games played on the estate. We were the Oliver Park outfit, or the 'Uppies'; the 'Downies' came from Weensland, and we always regarded them as being rough and tough. One of ours was a lovely guy called 'Tuff' Robson, who was a giant in those matches, big and strong, and a hell of a good player. We all wanted to be in his side, and when the teams were being picked, everybody would be looking to see who was going with him because he dominated everything. He always kicked the goals and had an amazing aptitude for driving the ball between the lamp-posts. Tuff eventually went on to play a couple of matches for Hawick, but was afterwards lost to rugby union when he moved to rugby league.

Happy days. It was a simple but wonderful upbringing.

My father, Murdoch McLaren, hailed from Bonhill in Dumbartonshire, but had moved to Hawick when he became a commercial traveller for the Innes Henderson knitwear company in the town, now known as Braemar Knitwear. He would be away from Monday to Friday, often visiting commercial outlets up in the north of Scotland, and I always missed him terribly. Remembering that, I always feel sad when I hear of families breaking up and children suddenly being denied the loving presence of both parents. All young boys want to see and be with their dads as much as possible.

Early every Monday morning, my father would make his way through the town to the railway station, and from our back garden we would watch his train puff its way out of Hawick in the direction of Edinburgh. I would stand forlornly, waving frantically as the sound of the train gradually faded into the distance. When the last wisps of smoke had disappeared out of sight around the bend and all was quiet, we would slowly retrace our steps back to the house. Then I'd collect my bag and set off for school.

I was lucky, though, that Father had a good job which enabled him to keep the family in comfort. I didn't want for much, even though life became much more difficult when my mother was struck down by illness.

Mother's maiden name was Margaret Helen Sutherland Guy, but she was known to one and all as Maggie. Tall and slim with big, brown eyes, she was a lovely lady. I have the fondest memories of her in her prime: she was a real character, and a very kind and thoughtful woman, too. She died in the mid-1950s.

I had two sisters, Jessie and Kit. Jessie was three or four years older than me, Kit a couple of years younger. Jessie was a great help when I was a boy. If I didn't have tuppence for the boys' paper *Hotspur*, she would invariably manage to scrape it together from somewhere. She was a very maternal sister, fortunately for me and Kit, as she had to look after us a lot when our mother's condition worsened. In Dad's absence during the week, Jessie did as much as she could to keep the family's lives running as smoothly as possible. I always had a great respect for her, and gratitude for all she did for us while we were growing up.

Kit was a runner, a really good athlete. She still lives in Hawick and was married to Ross Oliver, who played on the wing for Hawick and the South of Scotland. I got on pretty well with both my sisters and they both looked out for me, which I always appreciated.

Sunday lunch was the big meal of the week in our family, and it was sacrosanct. We would always have a roast on the table, and I remember my father carving off the slices from the joint, usually a leg of lamb, which was my favourite. During the week, I cycled home from school for lunch, so unlike many children then, I was eating good, basic food, meat and vegetables, every day.

I was thrilled when my father was appointed factory manager in Hawick and no longer had to travel round the country. It meant I could do a lot more with him. He introduced me to golf and stimulated my interest not only in that sport, but in rugby too. Most of my enthusiasm for sport was kindled by him. He taught me a lot of other things, too. Quite often on a Sunday morning, the pair of us would get up early, pack a snack and set off on a six- or seven-mile walk through the hills. About three miles out of Hawick, near Denholm, there used to be an orchard, and we might sit down there for a while in the morning sunshine, and Dad would tell me a story about rabbits or foxes. It was his way of introducing me to the lovely countryside in the Borders and all the beautiful walks so close to our home. We

Now here's a serious-looking wee fella! Note the pen in the jacket pocket. What was that scout's motto? 'Be Prepared'. (© BBC)

ABOVE: *Look at this mean-looking lot. It's the Hawick semi-junior XV, with its ultra-serious captain (yours truly, with ball) at 16 years old.*

BELOW: *Schooldays! My, they seem a wee while ago now. This is Classes IIIA and IIIB, July 1938, and I am second from left, front row.*

ABOVE: *The winners.
5 Medium Regiment,
Royal Artillery, at
Bolzano, Italy, February
1946. I am in my
lieutenant's uniform,
third from left in the
front row, seated next to
our brave leader, Colonel
'Crusher' Hayes.*

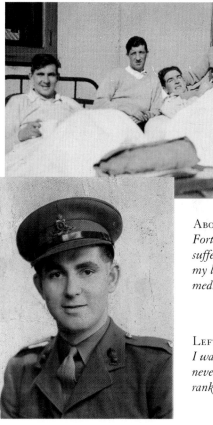

ABOVE: *With my pals in the East
Fortune Sanatorium, March 1949, whilst
suffering from TB. A miracle cure saved
my life and I'll always be grateful to the
medical staff for their heroic efforts.*

LEFT: *War over, 1945. By the end of it,
I was a temporary captain (they were
never very keen to give you permanent
rank!).*

ABOVE: *Bette and I together whilst I was in the isolation hospital. Her weekly visits gave me a reason to live when all had seemed lost.*

ABOVE: *What a catch! And the lovely bride wasn't half bad, either! Bette and I on our wedding day, March 1951.*

RIGHT: *With my beloved wife, indulging in another of my favourite sports, golf. What could make a man happier?*

ABOVE: *Our beautiful daughter Janie, who tragically died so young. It is still desperately hard for Bette and me to come to terms with her death.*

RIGHT: *Two lovely young ladies: Linda and Janie, aged 16 and 14. When they wore mini-skirts like this on holiday in Italy, I had to be right on my guard!*

ABOVE: *Our grandsons Gregor (left) and Rory.*

BELOW: *Our son-in-law Alan Lawson scoring one of his two tries for Scotland against England at Murrayfield, February 1976. Scotland won, 22–12. My, the BBC commentator was a proud man that day.* (© Offside)

LEFT: *The late, much loved Gordon Brown, Broon o' Troon, holding the Rugby World Cup. Gordon did so much for charity and was a marvellous man. His death at 52 was a tragedy.*
(© Colorsport)

BELOW: *'Are ye kidding, I've never swung a club like that in my life.' Taking lessons from legendary BBC golf commentator Peter Alliss.*
(© Empics)

ABOVE: *Proudly holding the MBE.* (© PA Photos)

BELOW: *Teaching duties at Hawick school. I loved working with the children and helping them to enjoy physical education.*
(both © Empics)

also played golf together, often with a friend of his, George Watters. As a boy, I was treated as an adult and I enjoyed that. Being able to do things with my dad and his friends was a rich experience for a young boy.

Everyday life then was very different. It was far more labour-intensive for a start: there was so much work involved just in running an ordinary family household. Yet there was a serenity to it that we seem to have lost today. Nothing was ever done at a hundred miles an hour; it was controlled and ordered and peaceful. Generally speaking, you didn't go rushing around very much because you didn't have the means to do so, either in practical terms or from the financial point of view. So there was a lovely pace to life, and you could be very happy with very little. Simple pleasures went a very long way. Like my new rugby ball that Christmas.

Right from the time when I was a wee boy, I had been taken to Mansfield Park, the home of the famous Hawick Rugby Football Club. It was like a pilgrimage for most families in the town. The day Father took his wee boy down to Mansfield Park for the first time was a red-letter day in the family history. Youngsters grew up steeped in the lore of the great club and the famous names who filled the ranks of its first XV. I had a tremendous interest in it from very early on and I think all the local boys were the same. When you were lining up a kick through the lamp-posts, you'd pretend you were the team's champion goal-kicker. If you scored a try, you'd be Hawick's flying wing. Schoolboys have a great capacity for improvisation and fantasy. It's a pity they can't always be as resourceful when it comes to algebra.

Coming from the west of Scotland, my father's roots were actually in soccer rather than rugby football – Donald Coleman, the Aberdeen FC trainer, was his cousin – but when he had come to live in Hawick he had immediately taken up rugby and became a real devotee of the game. My first sight of the players in the famous Hawick green jerseys came one Saturday afternoon when I was six. My wee hand clamped firmly in my father's, we walked briskly through the cold winter air to Mansfield Park to see a match. I think it was against Gala, our great local rivals, and I can still remember the spine-tingling excitement I felt when the two teams ran out on to the field. It was the start of a love affair with the game and the club that has lasted all my life.

There were huge crowds for all the big Hawick home games in those days. As many as 4,500 would make their way from the town centre along by the river to the ground, calling to one another, 'Aye, Jock, I think we'll nae be seeing too much running this afternoon, not with this rain.' Or, 'They cannae say it's no a good day for it.' I was in heaven. If you'd said, 'Here's a free ticket to Australia or Timbuctoo,' I wouldn't have swapped it for the chance to see a Hawick match. Two years later, in 1932, when I was still only eight, came the greatest adventure of my life. My dad took me up to Edinburgh to see Scotland play an international at my field of dreams: Murrayfield.

If I had thought going down the road through the town to see Hawick play was something special, then this was the equivalent of a journey to another planet. I was so excited I could hardly think of anything else in the week before the trip. Careful preparations had to be made. We had our tickets to the game – my dad must have got them from someone he knew through the club – but we had to be sure we had everything else needed on a day out up to Edinburgh. Sandwiches for lunch on the train, a snack and a drink, warm clothing for the long walk to and from the ground. We weren't so well off that we could just jump on and off buses whenever we felt like it. If there was a chance to save a few pennies by walking, then we did. I never thought twice about it.

I went to sleep that Friday night dreaming of walking down a long road and seeing a great vision in front of me. It was a rugby ground, and it was called Murrayfield. I knew that within twenty-four hours, that vision would become a reality.

Bright and early on the morning of 27 February 1932, we got up and dressed and made our way to the railway station. That day I hadn't even minded scrubbing my knees and putting on a clean shirt, normally the bane of all little boys' lives. For I was going to see Scotland play Ireland. At the station, we soon heard the whistle and whoosh of the train coming from Carlisle, on the English border, and bound for Edinburgh. Hissing and steaming like a giant snake, it drew into Hawick station and we clambered aboard. Like all little boys, I raced for the first available window seat and sat looking out, entranced.

The train picked up speed and pulled away from Hawick. The whistle blew as we rushed through little wooded sections of the line, or past frightened sheep out in the open fields on the hills. There was the comforting bumpety-bump, bumpety-bump of the tracks as we hurried over small bridges across rivers and streams, the smoke from the engine drifting past the window. I looked out at scenes of great beauty. Snow lay on the peaks of the tallest hills as we climbed higher and higher into the Border country, like a dusting of white icing sugar on a newly baked cake.

You couldn't have called the carriage luxurious by any means – the seats were simply hard, wooden benches – but to an eight-year-old on his first-ever visit to Edinburgh to see a rugby international, it mattered not a jot. We opened our basket and had some biscuits and a drink. Why is it all small boys immediately feel hungry when they begin a journey? As little stations and halts along the line came and went, my excitement mounted. My memories of the lovely scenery, the beautiful trees climbing up to the ridge of the skyline, were probably formed on later trips, because I'm sure I was too overwhelmed by the occasion to concentrate on it then. The land between the Borders and Edinburgh, the Scottish capital, is a wild part of the country, yet for all its remoteness and ruggedness, it has a raw beauty which, as I grew up, I came to appreciate more and more.

After about an hour and a half, the train slowed, crawled through a long tunnel and creaked, twisted and groaned its way into Edinburgh's Waverley station. There, it gave one final long hiss and stopped, and everyone got out.

I climbed the steps up from the station to see for the first time a sight visitors to Edinburgh from all over the world come to marvel at. Edinburgh Castle, perched high up on the hill. Below it lay Princes Street, the most famous thoroughfare in all of Scotland and, on this busy Saturday morning, filled with colour, sights and sounds. There were people out busy with their shopping, and others, like us, heading west in the general direction of Murrayfield.

Dad took my hand as we weaved through the crowds, towards the ground, a mile or two from the city centre. When we reached it, I looked up in wonderment at this great big stadium, the like of which I'd never seen. I don't remember there being the street sellers and hawkers you find outside any international rugby ground nowadays on match day. If you wanted a cup of tea, you had to bring it yourselves in a flask.

We took our seats in one grandstand – seats! This was luxury. There must have been 50,000 to 60,000 people in the stadium, and the cheer that went up when Scotland came out for the match has stayed with me ever since. In that team were three of 'our' forwards from Hawick: Jock Beattie, Willie Welsh and Jerry Foster. Like most people, I stood up and cheered, although I was too small to see everything round the big gentleman in front of us. I remember very clearly the sportsmanship of the crowd. Although they reacted to their own team doing well, I don't recall ever hearing any booing of the opposition or anything like that. Everyone was very disciplined. I think if anybody had booed, the fellow next to him would have had a quiet word with him.

In my commentating days, you may remember me occasionally remarking on any booing when a player was lining up a kick at goal. I have always hated that. I am a stickler for fair play and fair treatment of opposition players, and I am sure that is something I learned on trips such as the one that day to Murrayfield. My father was himself a great one for fair play, decency and for applauding the other side's achievements and seeing the other person's point of view. His attitude was to have a profound impact upon me when I came to commentate on Scotland's matches during my professional career and needed to remain strictly impartial. I like to think I succeeded in that, and I would also like to believe Dad would have thought so too and been proud of me.

Truth to tell, and perhaps not surprisingly, I don't remember an awful lot of the details of that match.

But I do know that it wasn't a happy day for us in terms of the outcome. Ireland won 20–8, a very heavy defeat for Scotland under the scoring system operating then, and the highest number of points Ireland had ever scored against the Scots. The history books recall that Scotland scored two tries, through centre George Wood and wing Max Simmers, but Ireland doubled that tally, and Paul Murray, their goal-kicking scrum-half, converted the lot. Six tries in one game wasn't a bad start to my rugby international-watching career. I was reared on the exploits of great rugby men like Simmers, G.P.S. MacPherson and Ian Smith, and another bonus for me that day was my first sight of Smith, the great wing known as the 'Flying Scot', after the famous train operating between London and Edinburgh. Ian, who represented Oxford University, Edinburgh University and London Scottish, was the darling of the Scottish rugby audiences at that time and my special hero, and it was a great thrill to see him in action. He was a big, powerful player with a high-stepping knee action that made him difficult to tackle.

Of course, in later years going up to Edinburgh for rugby matches was to become one of the regular features of my life. My secondary school, Hawick High School, had a regular fixture with Trinity

Academy, Edinburgh, played at Hawick one year, Edinburgh the next. It took place on the morning of an international match, so when it was in Edinburgh, we would get washed and changed after our match, have a meat pie and some lemonade and then go on to the international at Murrayfield in the afternoon. All the boys from both schools would try to get there early, and we'd all stand together down at the front of the terracing.

Once I became a commentator, I went to Murrayfield often, obviously, but there is nothing to beat your first experience of somewhere or something. Cricketers often tell you that the century they remember best is the first one they ever scored. I think it is the same with anything. It was special because I was with my father on a great day out, and my first taste of Edinburgh and Murrayfield. A very special day in my life, of that there can be no doubt.

I was to see plenty of other big matches as I grew up. As I've mentioned, in 1935, the New Zealand All Blacks came to Hawick to play the South of Scotland. Those New Zealanders did not run on to the pitch, they walked, following their captain, Jack Manchester, a huge man for those times, about six-foot-three and fifteen stone. Their quiet entrance only added to the sense of theatre and occasion at the ground that day. The man I would go on to work for in later years on the *Hawick Express* newspaper used to refer to them as 'prophets of doom'. That was about right, and I suppose it still is. You know you have one heck of a match in prospect when the All Blacks line up against you, even before they perform the traditional *haka*, the celebrated tribal war challenge laid down to all opponents before a game. In 1990, when Scotland played England for the Grand Slam in Edinburgh, David Sole led out his team in single file at a walking pace. It was claimed, erroneously, that this was the first time such an appearance had ever been made by a national rugby side, but those of us with longer memories could recall the All Blacks doing it some fifty-five years earlier. Not for nothing is it said that New Zealand is usually ahead of everyone else in the rugby world.

It was also in 1935 that I saw an England team play for the first time, again making the journey to Murrayfield with my father. Scotland won 10–7, their sixth successive victory over England in Edinburgh. Jock Beattie was the only representative of Hawick in the Scotland team that day. Then, a year later, when I was twelve, we saw another match against the auld enemy, this time at Twickenham.

In those days going to London really was some

trip. Nowadays many twelve-year-olds probably think no more of jumping on an aeroplane to France or Spain than they do of boarding a bus, but in 1936, London was a world away. Fortunately for us, my dad's two sisters, Ina and Kate, both lived there, working at the fashionable Harvey Nichols store, and so we had somewhere to stay. My father and I, accompanied by Uncle Joe, left for Hawick station late on the Friday evening – there was no skipping school for W.P. McLaren – to await the arrival of the night sleeper Pullman train from Edinburgh. There were quite a lot of other rugby supporters on the train, all heading for London to see the big game the next day.

The journey was immensely exciting. In our four-berth sleeping compartment we rattled and bumped our way south all night, crossing the border at Carlisle and calling at unfamiliar stations in England such as Preston, before rushing south through Lancashire and the Midlands and arriving at King's Cross at six in the morning. We had an early cup of tea and some biscuits on the train to fortify us for the last leg of the trip, across London to Twickenham.

I was far too busy absorbing all the sights and sounds of this thrilling, foreign city to feel the effects of the interrupted sleep of my night on the train. I gaped in awe at the busy traffic, the famous monuments and the sheer numbers of people on the streets as London gradually came to life on that Saturday morning. When you passed the end of a street, you would glimpse a sea of hats and caps as men and boys rushed about, carrying crates or pushing trolleys laden with all kinds of goods. There were ladies, too, dressed up in their finest long dresses and coats that reached almost to the ground.

But what astonished me the most as we made our way south-westwards was the absolute enormity of the city. The roads of the capital were by no means as smooth as billiard tables in those days, so we bumped and shook our way on hard, wooden bus seats all the way across it and out the other side until we finally reached Twickenham.

I was bowled over by the three huge stands rising in front of me, the great East and West stands, plus the old North Stand. This did not look like Murrayfield (which had only one stand in those days, and seemed a bit bare in comparison). It didn't feel like Murrayfield, either. The atmosphere was completely different. Elegantly dressed gentlemen sported fresh red roses in the lapels of their jackets. Some wore tweed suits that looked very smart indeed. There was a sense that we were close to the heart of the

Empire, and that there were important people all around you.

England were a powerful side and had just beaten New Zealand 13–0 at Twickenham, a match made famous by the dazzling skills of the legendary Prince Alexander Obolensky, the son of an officer in the Czar's Imperial Horse Guards, who had been brought to England as a baby to escape the Russian Revolution. He had scored two outstanding tries for the home team. The following year, 1937, England would win the Championship of the Four Home Unions (France had been expelled in 1931 for breaches of the rules on amateurism, and would not in the end be readmitted until after the war) by beating Scotland, Ireland and Wales. The day of my first visit to Twickenham, 21 March 1936, they were heavily favoured to beat Scotland, and duly did so, though only by 9–8, and only after one of the Scottish players, Rob Barrie from Hawick, broke his collarbone and had to leave the field. There were no substitutes allowed in those days, and Scotland had to accept their narrow defeat with fourteen men. They were led that day by Jock Beattie, who was winning his twenty-first cap. Jock was renowned for his strength – he worked at his family's joinery firm, Beattie & Sons, in Hawick – and was a bit bow-legged. I remember a spectator at Mansfield Park once shouting out during a club match: 'Hey, Jock, shut your legs – there's a train coming.'

Many years later, out walking one day in Hawick, I saw a figure gazing sadly into the river and thought I recognised it. I did: it was Jock Beattie, by then of course long since retired. I stopped to have a chat with him and I was glad afterwards that I did, for not all that much later he died. As a boy I had regarded Hawick and Scotland players like Jock and Willie Welsh as gods.

In 1938, we returned to Twickenham, where expectations of another England win in the Calcutta Cup were overturned by the play of Scotland's Wilson Shaw, a little flying machine of a fly-half. He scored two brilliant tries in front of a crowd of 70,000, one of which you wouldn't expect to see today because it was from the set piece, a scrum. Shaw got the ball travelling fast and flat, and normally a flank forward would have got to him, but that day he just carved his way through the England side, going at a real lick. I can still see him tearing up that left-hand side of the Twickenham pitch from our vantage-point in the East Stand. It seemed the whole of England was scattered by his magical footsteps that day. His two tries helped Scotland secure a

21–16 victory and with it the coveted Triple Crown.

I encountered Wilson Shaw again when I was a commentator and he was president of the Scottish Rugby Union. He was one of the first SRU committee men to acknowledge the media and actually co-operate with them. In the old days, the SRU were very suspicious of the press, and felt they should not be seen talking to us, so it was a real problem getting any information from them. But Wilson Shaw was a different type altogether, and there is no doubt he played a fundamental role in helping to make life easier for us working media men. He was a real gentleman as well.

Our weekend in London in 1938 was made memorable by Scotland's fine win. I was thrilled that I had been able to come to London again to witness it at first hand, because in those days, of course, it was the only way you could see a match: there was no television. If you couldn't be there, you might pick up a radio commentary if you were lucky; more likely just a brief report of the game.

We stayed with my aunts again, taking the train from Twickenham to central London and then a bus out to their home, and on the Sunday morning, set out for King's Cross and the long journey home to Scotland. I think we got back to Hawick around six that night.

Rugby filled my every waking moment. We moved from Weensland Road to Salisbury Avenue, where we had a back green about fifteen yards square, which I practised on, near my father's vegetable patch. Ingenuity was required here because of the risk of breaking a window, not to mention damaging my dad's prize vegetables. That would never have done. One day the inevitable happened and my magnificent, match-winning penalty goal for Scotland flew straight into a window. There was an awful crack and I knew I was for it. My punishment was an extra spoonful a day of cod-liver oil, the awful stuff adults used to force down the throats of their offspring in what I as a young lad considered a thoroughly misguided attempt to keep us all healthy.

After that, I made paper balls to practise with, tying wads of paper into the shape of a rugby ball with string. It might have looked a bit humble, but at least no more windows got broken and it didn't affect the results of the 'matches'. England never had a sniff of a win in my games against them. I would kick off for Scotland, catch the ball for England, running it down the back line before it was dropped. That would be Scotland's chance. I would quickly change sides again, rushing towards the end I had just been defending, and the ball would be transferred through the hands of the backs at the speed of light for a Scotland wing named W.P. McLaren to touch down in the corner, the Scotland centre, W.P. McLaren, having given him the scoring pass at just the right moment. Poor old England took some terrible poundings. On one occasion Scotland won 73–3. That was a red-letter day indeed for the boys in the dark blue jerseys.

When I look back, I wonder whether there was enough variety to my life as a boy. I never really visited many art galleries or museums or saw any of the other great European cities such as Paris, Amsterdam, Stockholm or Madrid. But in those days few people travelled very far. Visits to Edinburgh were rare, and to London rarer still, and you certainly couldn't catch a plane and be in Paris in an hour or two. You were content to live out your life in your home surroundings, with family and friends close by. Money was tight in many homes, mine included, and there just weren't the spare pennies to fund constant trips. In the summer, we might go to the coast for a week's holiday, and just seeing the sea was an enormous highlight of my childhood. We lived a far more intimate, cloistered life than children today, and we did not hanker for ever greater delights or glamorous locations because what you've never had, you don't miss.

Mind you, we had great fun, and we were right wee rascals, too. I have a picture of myself at nine or ten in which I look like a miniature Al Capone. One of our pranks involved attaching a bit of thread to a little pin, and tying a wee stone on to the end of the thread. We would use this stone to cause all manner of nuisance. We might knock it against someone's window to make the occupant pull back the curtain and peer out. Seeing nothing (we lads would be hiding in the bushes), he or she would go away. Another tug on the thread, and the stone would knock against the window again. Again, a face would appear at the window, peering suspiciously up and down the street. In the bushes, we'd be almost bursting with laughter at our own cleverness. After the third knock at the window our victim would come outside to look up and down the road. Then he or she might see the stone and the thread attached to it, but by then we'd be well away, having made a run for it.

Sometimes I got more than I bargained for. Noticing one autumn day that the luscious-looking pears in our next-door neighbour's garden were just about ripe and ready to eat, I decided I should be the one doing the eating. But I underestimated the difficulty of getting my grubby little hands on them. I gingerly climbed up the fence and into the pear tree, and was just about to reach out for a large, juicy pear when the branch broke and I went tumbling out of the tree and down a fifty-foot embankment. I fell into a clump of blackberry bushes and stinging nettles. Talk about forbidden fruit. I went home, tail firmly between my legs, covered in scratches.

'What on earth happened to you?' my mother said.

'Oh, I fell over,' I replied, all casual like.

But I never went up that tree again.

I was not inclined to get into the local baker's van any more, either. At the age of nine or ten, like most small boys, I was fascinated by motor vehicles. When the baker hopped out of his van to deliver his bread, pies and pastries, I liked to hop in and sit in the driver's seat. I'd pretend to be turning the wheel, like a Grand Prix racing driver hurtling around a track. It was great fun. Or at least it was until the day the van took off with me in it.

I didn't understand what was happening, but it seems that I must have leaned forward and accidentally released the handbrake. The next thing I knew, the van started to trundle slowly down a small incline near our house, heading straight for a fence. I held on to the steering wheel for dear life – suddenly, driving didn't seem so much fun as it had before. The van came to rest against the fence, its front offside wing bearing a long scrape. The baker was very good about it – he seemed concerned about whether I was hurt rather than angry – but I knew I'd catch hell when my father got to hear about it.

One of my quieter, safer activities was helping one of our distant relations, Frank Anderson, shepherd his cows into a field he owned not far from our home. I used to like going down there and lending a hand. It was nice being out in the open air and working with animals. I'd stand behind the cows and try to shoo them into the appropriate place. Occasionally I'd go down to our local livestock market and assist the men with moving the sheep from one pen to the other. There was always a buzz about the town on market day. The farmers would come in from the nearby hills to sell or buy flocks of sheep and the marketplace was alive with the bleats of the sheep, the shouts of the bidders and the monotone voice of the auctioneer calling out the bids and prices. It was a good way to fill a spare morning and the people who worked there were always glad of an extra pair of hands.

We lads amused and entertained ourselves through our own ideas and ingenuity. We didn't have to wait to be told what to do, or be taken somewhere. Nor, of course, did we sit glassy-eyed in front of a television set for hours on end, for the very good reason that we didn't have television. Whether it did us more good not having it I don't know, but I do think it helped us think for ourselves more and made us more creative.

Our parents were stricter then, too, and gave us firm guidelines that had to be adhered to. We were set upon the path of good behaviour in a more serious way than is the case today. There were certain things you were careful about, for example, like not trampling people's gardens when you were going to retrieve a ball. You had to show respect for what belonged to others, which was no bad thing. So when our ball was hoofed into a neighbour's garden we were all very thoughtful about how we got it back and made sure the ground was levelled afterwards and not left with footprints all over it.

The social structure that underpinned our lives in those days established clear parameters that helped us recognise right from wrong. Of course, pushing boundaries is human nature, and there is nothing wrong with that, but we knew pretty much what would be tolerated, not just by our parents but by the world at large. If we strayed too far from the straight and narrow, our parents would come down on us like a ton of bricks. But that wasn't required very often.

Living in Hawick, it was easy to live and dream rugby football, for the game was the constant topic of conversation among almost everyone, men and women, in the town and it gave them a strong cultural identity. When I was old enough to play for the club, people used to come up to me and ask how I was doing in 'their' team. You wore the famous green jersey like a badge of honour. Every Scottish Border town is proud of its own identity, and nothing can be allowed to tarnish it. Hawick people are Hawick people and Gala folk, Gala folk – each proud of their town's traditions.

Each town has its annual festival, and Hawick's is known as the Common Riding. It is held on the weekend after the first Monday in June, when our horsemen, spearheaded by a young man appointed as leader, ride out to check that the boundaries of the town are secure and that no enemy has been there. It is a tradition that commemorates the exploits of a group of young fellows, or 'callants', in 1514, the year after the Battle of Flodden, in which James IV of Scotland was killed. These local heroes raided the camp of a band of English soldiers from Hexham at Hornshole, three miles down the road, captured the troop's banner, the 'Hexham Pennant', and carried it victoriously back to Hawick.

Sometimes as many as sixty young riders, led by a young man called the cornet, take part, galloping around the countryside and up to all the high points, including the hill near our golf course, which over-looks the town. The schoolchildren are given the Thursday and Friday off, which of course makes it a hugely popular event with them. The fair comes to Hawick, and families go up on to the moor, known as the Hillside, where there are horse races and all sorts of activities for the kids, a communal picnic – and a good deal of beer-swilling as well. You might see 5,000 people up there that weekend, all enjoying themselves.

When I was a boy, the Common Riding was a highlight of the year. I remember there used to be an old chap down our way who would throw coins out so that the youngsters could have a scramble for the money, which itself became something of a tradition. As a promising wing forward, I was always there, close to the ground. However, I never had a great desire to be a cornet. I'd been put off horses by an incident that took place when I was about eight or nine, at Silloth, a lovely spot on the Solway Firth where we used to go for our annual family holiday.

On the beach there they had donkey and pony rides for the children. On this holiday, I am told, when I was offered a donkey ride, I pulled a face, had a wee stamp (you wouldn't believe it now, looking at me, would you?) and insisted that I didn't want a donkey, I wanted a proper horse. 'Are you quite sure you can handle it?' my father asked.

'Of course,' I replied petulantly.

Well, they got me up on this horse and I suppose the animal sensed the presence on its back of a right Charlie who didn't have much of a clue. No sooner had I clambered aboard than it took off, charging up the beach and right down the main street, with me hanging on for dear life. I was petrified. All I could do was just cling on to its neck. If I'd had a gun, I would happily have shot it, I can tell you. At last somebody stopped the wretched thing, and I was lifted off, sound in limb but in a state of shock. So by the grand old age of ten I'd decided I'd done all the charging around on a horse I ever wanted to.

Borders folk who have moved away never lose their love for their native town, and the Common Riding weekend regularly attracts two or three hundred exiles from Hawick. They might come home only once every ten years, but when they do, it is invariably for the festival. Indeed, it has become such a feature of the weekend that a big gathering in the Town Hall is arranged specially for them. It is very moving to see these people from all over the world returning to the place where they clearly still feel their lives are rooted, and many tears are shed. I wonder what our ancestors would make of it all today? What would they think of their deed being remembered after all this time – the better part of five hundred years – not to mention being celebrated by Hawick folk now scattered around the globe?

As well as the Common Riding, the Olympic Games were held in Hawick. Och aye, ye didnae know that? Where were you? The Olympics were hosted there almost every week. Great athletes from all over the world would descend on our town, on our street, in fact. There was just enough room there to fit in the track for the 100-yard sprint before the lamp-posts or someone's front door got in the way; hurdle races were set up using refuse buckets and old fruit crates. And I would sit on the wall and commentate on it all.

'You're very welcome to Hawick and this first day of competition at the 1935 Olympic Games. There is a terrific battle in prospect here today between Jardine of the United States, Walker of England, two flying Frenchmen, the German Strauber and the Scot, Henderson. It looks like a classic hundred yards

Olympic final and, ladies and gentlemen, they're on their marks, ready to go . . .'

The sound of a 'boom', like a gun starting, would then be heard down our road.

'. . . and they're off, and it's a great start by Jardine for the United States, but Henderson has gone with him and Strauber, the German, is close. Halfway down the straight, and Henderson is closing all the time, Strauber can't find any more and Jardine looks as though he's tiring. Twenty yards to go, Henderson noses in front, it's Henderson, flying for the line, and Henderson is the Olympic Champion!'

Sometimes on a Friday afternoon after school, my father would come round the corner on his way back from work and stand there and listen to me finishing my commentary on the big race. I suppose he wanted to know who would win! He never dissuaded me from my hobby. Who knows where I developed the interest? I was only around eleven or twelve at that time and there was no connection whatsoever in our family with the media. I had never thought about becoming a sportswriter, or anything like that, when I grew up. Indeed, writing about sport never particularly appealed to me, just commentating. I wanted to be a teacher. There were signs of that future, too, in those street Olympics. As well as doing the commentaries I would be organising the events, putting up the hurdles and arranging the races. But I never dreamed I would actually end up as a sports commentator, still less one specialising in the game I loved. It would have been beyond the wildest fantasy of even a sports-mad child.

I liked to impersonate the commentators of the day, like Howard Marshall and H.B.T. Wakelam. Marshall had the awfully nice, upper-class English accent typical of the BBC then – everybody on the wireless, as it was called in those days, spoke like that, and little concession was made to regional accents. In later years, when I was with the BBC myself, my father reminded me of the times he used to come home from his work and hear me up the stairs in the spare room, practising. I used to plan out a fictional game on big double foolscap sheets and commentate on the entire match, describing all the imaginary scores and phases of play. I have always been happy that both my parents took great pride in what I was doing when I began commentating in real life, and I was proud because they were proud. I think that is the natural way for parents and children. My father was around to see me commentating in real life for many years – he lived to the age of ninety-two – and for the BBC, too, a revered corporation with an enviable reputation the world over, which pleased him.

I did all right at school, passing adequately in the key subjects. As for my favourite subject, that was rugby, followed closely by rugby. And after that? Well, I loved gym, especially going over the box and the horse, and climbing the ropes. I did quite like French, but as luck would have it, one of our French periods was always on a Wednesday afternoon, just before games, and I always suspected the French teacher, a small, dumpy lady called Vera Fisher, of punishing us for bad behaviour or for not doing our work well enough by delaying us in getting out to play rugby. There was no greater crime in my book, and I developed an unreasonable dislike of her. Even so, my French became quite good in the end, and in the long run I had every reason to be grateful to Vera, as it came in very handy at French rugby training sessions. Their officials were always more helpful if you could speak a bit of their language. At the time, however, I was not amused.

I also liked science, though that probably had more to do with the teacher than the subject. Jack Frame played centre for Hawick and I hero-worshipped him. Imagine my pride and pleasure then when, at the age of seventeen, I was picked alongside him for

Hawick in two or three first-team games. It was unusual for a teacher and pupil to be appearing together in a senior club side. I was a stand-off half or centre early on; it was only when I played a bit of rugby in the Army that I switched to flank forward.

Many years later, I had to go up to Kirkcaldy in the Scottish midlands to cover a cup match for BBC Scotland radio. Jack Frame was by then living in Kirkcaldy, and I met up with him. He gave me a lot of useful background information on the local side which I was able to use for my commentary.

Overall, I don't think education was regarded as the be-all and end-all in those days, as it is today. Certainly no one stood in the way of me playing an awful lot of rugby. I suppose most of my teachers would have considered that I didn't reach my full potential and it's doubtless true that I could have done better. I slogged away at the other academic subjects, mathematics, history, geography and art, but once I got home from school and caught sight of a rugby ball, everything else paled into insignificance. I was made to do my homework all right, and I read my books, but it was only when I went out on to that patch of grass or our back green and felt that wonderful leather ball in my hands that I was in my real element.

CHAPTER 6

JOURNALISM
AND
TEACHING

WHEN I CAME OUT OF THE SANATORIUM, MY LIFE saved by that new wonder drug, I faced a very different future from the one I had been looking forward to before I went in. My rugby career was over. I had to accept that after such a debilitating illness I would never again be able to play at a level that would give me any hope of realising my ambition to pull on the Scotland jersey. I was in despair for a time over that, mourning the Scotland cap I had been so close to winning when the TB struck. Now all that was in the past, and I had to rebuild my life. It was a daunting task.

I had been receiving a pension from the Army because my ill health was attributable to war service, but that would not continue for much longer. I had my PE qualification from Aberdeen under my belt, and I wanted to use that to teach, as I had originally intended, but there were two problems. The first was that you were not allowed to take up a teaching post so soon after suffering from TB. There was always a fear that it might come back, and you might be infectious, so you had effectively to place yourself in quarantine for a good two or three years. You also had to be careful that you didn't ever let yourself get too cold – not easy for a PE teacher.

The second restriction was that I wasn't keen on moving far from Hawick to work. I had met Bette on 17 March 1947 and we had rapidly become close, but then came the TB. Even when I eventually left hospital I had to convalesce for a year, so we didn't get married until 22 March 1951. The Revd Henry M. Cook married us at the Hawick Congregational Church and we held the reception at the Tower Hotel, with about eighty guests. Ideally we wanted to make our home in Hawick, but there were practical considerations, too. When I left the sanatorium all my X-rays and case-history notes were sent to my local doctor. I didn't fancy the idea of living up in Aberdeen or somewhere, falling ill and finding that all my notes were in Hawick. So I decided to wait for a position as a teacher of physical education to become available in Hawick. That wait was to last nine years.

In the meantime, I answered an advertisement for a junior reporter on the local newspaper, the *Hawick Express*. That application was to change my entire life. I was called for an interview, and shortly afterwards I received a letter to say that I had got the job. I was to report to the newspaper's offices down a little alleyway just off the High Street the following Monday morning, which I duly did.

The job on the paper was something I only ever saw as a means to earn some money, but I came to enjoy it a great deal. Mind you, it was very hard work. I don't think I could ever be accused of being a 'natural journalist'. I probably wasn't aggressive or cheeky enough to survive a lifetime in that competitive business. It involves living on your wits and nerves under pressure and the many friends I have made in journalism over the years have all subscribed to the theory that it might not be the best career to choose if you want a long life. Admittedly, working on a local paper in Hawick does not compare with working on one of the big national newspapers in London, Edinburgh or Glasgow, but all the same, it was quite a slog.

On a local newspaper in those days you were expected to cover everything: council meetings, Education Committee meetings and any other important gatherings; fires, burglaries and police activities. Being a young reporter and keen to impress, I was not particularly worried about my own health and safety. I remember once rushing off to a big fire which had broken out in a hosiery factory and unwittingly standing too close to the blazing building. I very nearly got burned myself when part of it toppled down, sending lumps of flaming wood and debris flying past me. I hadn't realised until then just how much heat was being generated by this huge fire. It practically took the skin off my face.

The best part was being given the chance to write on rugby. Going to Mansfield Park had been one of my greatest pleasures for as long as I could remember, and now, astonishingly, I was being paid to go and sit in the press box at the ground, watch the match, talk to the players and committee men before and after the game and record all the statistics I would need. The appropriate analogy here would be the one about a pig wallowing in mud. For me it was paradise, and I couldn't have been happier.

My brief was to cover Hawick's first-team games, the South of Scotland matches and also the junior fixtures played in the town. That entailed reporting on virtually every Hawick match for what turned out to be the best part of nine seasons. I could never have guessed, or dared to dream at that stage that I was destined to spend so much of my life in close proximity to a rugby ball and to rugby folk. It only happened because one man, quite unbeknown to me, happened to make a telephone call to a business contact.

That man was my boss, John Hood, the editor of the *Hawick Express*, who was also the BBC's representative in the Borders. He mentioned to someone at the BBC that he had a young fellow on his staff who did a lot of record-keeping on rugby and might make a good commentator. Oh, and he was very keen on the game.

One day Mr Hood called me into his office, told me about this phone call and inquired as to whether I had heard anything from the BBC. I thought he was joking. But in fact a letter had arrived at my home some time before, addressed to me, on BBC headed paper, asking me to attend a commentary audition at the match between the South of Scotland and the touring 1951–2 Springboks at Mansfield Park. I didn't know anybody at the BBC, and I'd taken one look at it and decided that either it had been sent to me by mistake or someone was having me on. It began to dawn on me now that it had been genuine, and I was scared stiff.

'Me? Do a proper audition for the BBC? No fear. I'm not going.'

'You are,' growled Mr Hood.

And he practically frog-marched me down to Mansfield Park to do it.

There were five other candidates and we were all asked to do ten minutes each. That was no problem for me, as I'd been doing imaginary commentaries on rugby matches for so long that it was almost second nature. The BBC, in the shape of Peter Thomson and Archie Henry, two of their luminaries in Scotland, must have seen some potential in me because I was the lucky one invited back for a second audition. Three weeks later, I did another test commentary, this time on Heriot's FP against Watsonians in Edinburgh. Then in December 1952 came the crunch: I was asked to provide a live commentary, lasting fifty-five minutes, on an inter-city match between Glasgow and Edinburgh, to be broadcast on the Scottish Home Service.

Of course, I took it all in my stride: I hardly ate for two days beforehand, could barely pack my bag properly for the match, my hands were shaking so much, and I got to the ground absolutely hours before I needed to be there, just in case ... By the time I was linked into the programme via my head-phones, I was a nervous wreck. I was convinced every listener would hear a strange banging coming down the line from Glasgow: my poor heart thump-ing away. But I soon came to realise that this anxiety was all part of the build-up. Indeed, if you didn't feel somewhat nervous and unsettled, then you probably wouldn't produce a very good commentary. It was to give me an edge, that nervousness, throughout my career.

I wondered whether it was simply my rugby back-ground, my knowledge of the game, its players and its traditions, that had appealed to the BBC. I could explain the laws to the listeners, too. They must have decided that I was also capable of developing the skills needed to describe immediate events clearly over the microphone, because on the strength of that acid test of the live commentary, they took me on.

I was shocked when I first heard myself on radio: my voice sounded so slow and sleepy. I didn't realise that you had to keep pace with play, and that that involved being spot-on with your description of what was happening. But I was lucky in that my voice did seem to come over distinctly. I was surprised and pleased at the number of older people who stopped me in the street and said, 'Hey, Billy, we did enjoy your commentary – we could hear every word.' I won't tell you about some of the other things they said! Only joking . . .

During the week, I was working for the *Hawick Express* all day, plus evenings when there was a meeting to be covered, and until my BBC job started, most Saturdays, too, with the occasional junior match on a Sunday. It didn't leave a lot of time for life with my new wife.

I was lucky in that Bette was a dream in that respect. It can't have been much fun for a young married lady having to put up with a husband who would sit down to eat his dinner at home and, on hearing the fire siren, suddenly leap up and dash off to report on whatever was going on. I think many a time most of my dinner went into the bin, or had to be kept for later that night when I eventually got back. But that was the life of a local newspaper man. One week it might be endless meetings, the next a series of fêtes or school sports events (and woe betide you if you got the names wrong, the ages wrong or mixed up people in a group photograph taken by the paper's resident photographer).

But I found it an interesting life because there was so much variety. The sport, of course, always fascinated me, and when the rugby season was over there would be tennis events, cricket matches and golf tournaments. Often I would go to the golf course after doing a full day's work at the office to get all the details of that day's competition. Then I had to ride my bicycle all the way back again and sit in a lonely office typing up the news for the next morning. I might also have to send a report of the tournament to the national newspapers, for which we did quite a bit of freelance work through their Scottish offices. After a while, a Morris 12, which I regarded as a great brute of a motor car, replaced the bicycle and made life a little easier, though I seem to remember it was very heavy on petrol.

Life went on for me over the years in this way, working for the *Hawick Express* and developing my commentating career with the BBC. I was content, but I have to say I never lost sight of my desire one day to take up that teaching career. In my heart of hearts I had always wanted to be a teacher, though to date my only experience of the job had been a four-week stint during my training at my old primary school, Trinity Primary. I had never dreamed it would be such a long time before I would be able to resume my career.

In the meantime Bette had presented me with two

beautiful daughters. Linda was our first born, in 1952, followed two years later by Janie. I was thrilled by their arrival. Being a father brought extra responsibilities, but I felt that to have children fulfilled the whole meaning of marriage. Bette and I were as pleased as Punch the day we brought each baby daughter home from the local hospital. Bedrooms were decorated and filled with toys and furniture. Our lives had taken on a completely new dimension.

The joy the children brought us both as they grew up was inestimable, and the fun was endless. Bette told me once that when I first appeared on television, the girls sat in front of the set waving frantically and sticking their tongues out at me, as naughty little girls are wont to do. They seemed upset when I didn't do the same back to them.

The joke was often on me. On a family walk in the country one day we came to this small wall with a wire running round the front of it. Someone said, 'That might be an electric fence,' but I was determined it was not going to stop me going over the wall. I must have slipped, and somehow caught my head on this wire, and the next thing I knew I was reeling from an electric shock. My family were a great source of comfort to me. They were all doubled up with laughter.

When the girls were small I was always terrified some harm might come to them. We went down to Scarborough on the east coast of England on holiday one year. It was a delightful town, but what Linda and Janie remembered most about it was my fear of letting them out of my sight in case they fell into the harbour. They told me years later that I virtually had them by the neck in an armlock. I suppose I felt it might have been a bit tricky explaining to Bette what had happened to the girls if something went wrong.

'Where are the children, Bill?'

'Oh, they just dropped into the water a wee while ago. I expect they'll be along in a moment . . .'

At last, in 1959, I heard that a vacancy for a PE teacher had arisen in Hawick. I immediately applied and was thrilled to get the job. I felt I was more than ready for a new challenge, and the fact that it was so close to home was a real bonus. The post covered four primary schools – three in the town and one on the outskirts – plus Hawick High School. Two of these schools, Trinity Primary and Hawick High, I had attended myself. Now I would be teaching the sons of men I had been to school with or played alongside at Mansfield Park. Being involved at both primary and secondary levels also meant I would be working with some pupils throughout their school lives. So in addition to the practical considerations, teaching in Hawick also offered me a rewarding sense of continuity. It was ideal in every way.

Although I had enjoyed my time with the *Hawick Express*, facing the end of my journalistic career gave me little cause for dismay. However, it was on the paper that I had come under the wing of my first boss, John Hood, who was an outstanding human being and a great role model for me. He was hard but fair; disciplined but a man who always considered others, and he did a great deal to help his protégés along their way – all qualities that I knew I needed to take with me if I was ever to become a really successful teacher.

It was John Hood, of course, who had got my broadcasting career off the ground, and that did turn out to be a great help to a games master. When I came back from an international rugby weekend to take a group of fifty or sixty boys for a rugby practice session, I was able to draw on the lessons from that match. I'd say, 'Well, last Saturday at the game, this happened or that took place.' It made practice interesting for the boys. I think they liked to feel they were doing the same things that Scotland, England or France had been doing in the international arena. It helped to capture their attention.

The Education Committee must have thought so, because they were very generous and understanding over the years in giving me time off to prepare for my BBC role. I was extremely lucky in that respect. I could not have had kinder employers.

My timetable was drawn up by the director of education. I was at Drumlanrig Primary School, where I was based, on Tuesday morning. I went to Wilton Primary School on a Wednesday morning, returning to Drumlanrig in the afternoon, and spent three afternoons a week at Hawick High School, helping out with the senior boys' games. Trinity and Burnfoot I fitted in during the remainder of the week. I enjoyed the mix of senior and primary students, and the continuity of picking up the threads with children I'd taught at the various primary schools when they graduated to Hawick High School.

I know that in England, PE teachers often took classes in academic subjects as well, and certainly schools didn't employ specialists at primary level, but in Scotland, physical education stood on its own and because my job covered five schools I didn't teach anything else. I loved going to the primary schools because the kids were so enthusiastic. They were always just dying to get into the gym to burn off some of that surplus energy and they saw their gym lessons as a break from the classroom. The gym was for fun, so my classes were very popular. We would get them down the stairs, changed and ready to go quickly and have around thirty-five minutes with them. Discipline was vital and you had to be aware of everything that was going on. Classes were big in those days – you might be responsible for anything from thirty-five to forty-five pupils – and accidents can happen in a gym, especially if you have six different groups working at different activities, with people up wall bars, ropes swinging round and people jumping over boxes. So you had to be on your toes. I always put great emphasis on safety and would stand close to the piece of equipment I considered carried most risk. There were always one or two daredevils you had to keep your peepers on to make sure they didn't end up in hospital, but generally, we were pretty lucky and didn't have many injuries, apart from one wee laddie once breaking his arm as he came off a beam awkwardly.

In the summertime, we were able to be outside more. There would be cricket and tennis and I would organise athletics events. We would have triangular competitions with other local schools and the results were published by my old pals at the *Hawick Express*.

What I loved about teaching was seeing youngsters working things out for themselves. I did not believe in imposing so tight a structure that they did not need to do that. My aim was to provide a basic formula and encourage them to adapt it to suit their own capabilities and requirements. It was fascinating to stand back and watch how different children handled this challenge. I regarded physical education as an opportunity to give young people a good all-round experience and preparation for life in general. Above all, I wanted to see them achieve. That gave me more satisfaction and pleasure than anything else. Even wee things. For example, I loved being there when a child who had been a shade frightened about leaping over the high horse cleared it for the first time. You could sense him puffing out his chest with pride at his success. It was exhilarating to be able to initiate that kind of effort in young people, and I felt I had achieved something myself when something like that happened.

When it came to coaching rugby, I was in my element, of course. We held training sessions at Wilton Park, which had five or six sets of rugby posts and changing rooms, too. On Saturday mornings, we would play inter-school matches. Some fine players of the future passed through our hands in Hawick,

Scotland internationals like Tony Stanger, Alastair Cranston, Colin Deans, Jim Renwick, Ian Barnes, Alister Campbell, Keith Murray, Brian Hegarty and Greig Oliver. Tony Stanger, the Scottish wing who scored the crucial try in the 1990 Grand Slam showdown win over England at Murrayfield, was, to be frank, a bit of a nuisance as a youngster. At primary school he was already so big and strong that sometimes I had to tackle him myself to help out the smaller boys. Seriously, though, he was a most likeable lad. He had a genuine talent and he was modest with it.

Jim Renwick was one of my star pupils. I remember him at ten, a lad who always had an impish touch. Jim was to go on to become one of the finest centres in Scottish rugby history, and he played for the British Lions in South Africa in 1980. Few could match him for talent, pace or guile, and he was brave, too.

Alastair Cranston was also a product of Hawick High School. He was a country boy, as strong as a bullock. Then there was Colin Deans, a prize pupil who was as fast a hooker on the school rugby field as I can recall. His father Peter had played in the same Hawick side as I did, so it was especially pleasing to coach his son. Alister Campbell I taught at both Burnfoot Primary and Hawick High.

Today I am a life member of Hawick RFC and it gives me enormous satisfaction when I think of all the young players I have helped, in some small way, to come through the system and give long years of service to what is one of the great clubs of world rugby.

It always gave me a frisson of excitement to see on the rugby field a boy I sensed would go all the way to the top. In a training match between two groups one day, one eleven-year-old caught my attention almost the first time he received the ball. He took it confidently, and somehow he seemed to have more time at his disposal than his team-mates. There was something else, too: an apparently natural understanding of what he should do with it which marked him out as special.

When the play broke down, I asked him what his name was. 'Craig Chalmers, sir,' he replied in a crisp, self-assured tone. I knew I had seen a rare talent that day, and I wasn't wrong. Craig joined Melrose when he was old enough and went on to play sixty times for Scotland between 1989 and 1999. He was a part of the Grand Slam team of 1990 and also became a British Lion in New Zealand in 1993.

Of course, it doesn't automatically follow that a bright talent will translate into success. Young players had to work on all parts of their game, not only their skills but also discipline, fitness, determination and concentration. But those who showed the application to match their innate ability were a source of huge pride to their rugby master.

Teaching in those days was far easier than it is now because for the most part the children were so much more obedient. Dividing lines were clearly drawn, at home and school alike, and children knew what they could and could not get away with. If they did something that was not allowed, the majority took their punishment, and certainly their parents were generally on the teacher's side.

In my own schooldays, you knew what to expect if you were caught playing the fool, or breaking the rules. I can recall as an eleven-year-old getting six of the best from my headmaster, along with one of my chums. I've long since forgotten what it was for, but I remember the six whacks very well. There we were, Master Robert Thomson and Master William McLaren, standing with our heads down, awaiting our turn to get the belt. When I got back to my place, I put my hands on the cold, metal upright of the desk to try to get a bit of relief from the burning pain.

To us, physical discipline was an occupational hazard. Something to be avoided if at all possible, but probably inevitable from time to time. You took your punishment without complaint.

As a schoolteacher, I derived no great satisfaction from punishing pupils for misbehaviour, nor did I think it was ever acceptable for a teacher to lose his or her temper with a child. Punishment was accepted if it was meted out in a proper, controlled manner. Throughout my teaching career, I used the belt – the strap some called it – a few times, but I never hit a child in any other circumstances.

Now that corporal punishment is illegal, it is much harder for teachers to control their pupils. Without the threat of punishment as a deterrent, there are very few options available to the teacher. There are staff in schools who are frightened to enforce what disciplinary action is allowed because they fear where it might end. They must be so careful about any physical contact in particular. We have all read reports of recent cases in which a teacher has been up in court, charged with assault, and his or her whole career has been on the line. Very often, the courts have backed the teacher's explanation and thrown out such cases, but it must be nerve-racking, not to say soul-destroying, all the same.

I loved teaching – and I continued to teach until I was sixty-five, in 1989 – but I don't think I would like it today. This weakening of the powers of our educators has left them with an almost impossible task. It must be like trying to do your job with one hand tied behind your back. They have to take the cheek, smart quips and rudeness of their pupils, some of whom, let us be honest, are not interested in learning anything at school or in getting on in life. It is those who do want to learn who suffer under the modern system. If you had the authority to use proper disciplinary measures – and yes, I would include physical punishment among them – you would have some means of isolating the trouble-makers and acting to stop them influencing the rest of the class.

In my view there will be a serious long-term cost to this damaging policy, and it is a bleak prospect. The whole structure of society over the last hundred years or more has been built upon young people respecting their parents, teachers and police officers. Without that – and already children are growing up with no regard for these three institutions – what are we left with? I sometimes wonder whether there is a way that we can reintroduce some discipline into the lives of our young people. I don't see anything terribly wrong with a system of authority based to some extent on fear. As small boys at Trinity Primary in

Hawick, we were in awe of our headmaster, Mr Burns. We knew that if we did something wrong, we would be punished, and that knowledge alone was enough to lend the head an aura which persuaded you to keep on the right side of him more often than not. You paid attention to what he said, and if he was speaking, you concentrated and learned from him. I'm not saying it was essential for pupils to be afraid of teachers, but a sense of caution, an awareness of the consequences of crossing established boundaries, was no bad thing. If a pupil was a little wary of a teacher, the chances were that it was this teacher from whom the child would learn the most.

Of course, you cannot have teachers going over the top and dishing out physical punishment without clear guidelines. But if you take away that option altogether, you have removed from the entire teaching profession any possible deterrent, which means you are asking children to discipline themselves. I'm sorry, but I just don't believe they are capable of that. I have always believed a strong hand was a prerequisite for keeping errant pupils in line. You would start in the nicest way, pointing out the consequences of bad behaviour, and in my experience, most of the time that solved the problem. If it didn't, you needed to have some method of punishment available to you.

There is arguably a greater need for discipline in schools nowadays because not all parents are setting proper standards at home. Raising a family is extremely time-consuming, and for one reason or another – the pressures of demanding jobs, or simply because they are unwilling to make sacrifices in other areas of their lives to devote greater care and attention to their children – some parents don't seem to have the time to do the job properly and appear to feel it appropriate to leave the matter of teaching their offspring right from wrong to the schools. This is something that should be handled by parents and teachers in partnership. Sadly, though, the reality is that often parents won't accept criticism of their child. When I was a boy, if a teacher told me off, I made sure I kept quiet about it at home, because if my parents found out they would give me more of the same. Today's parents are just as likely to go straight to the school and complain about any punishment meted out.

Children need guidance to come to an understanding of how far they can and cannot go. Take that away and they are floundering, doing what they want and respecting no one in their lives in the belief that they are not constrained by rules. Inevitably some will take a wrong turning without even recognising it as such. The poor standards of behaviour we see today are a consequence of this breakdown of discipline. Society is reaping a bitter harvest from its absurd policy of toleration at all times of all things. We are simply not being fair to our young people.

The fragmentation of families is another major issue that affects children deeply and with which teachers increasingly have to contend on a large scale. Divorce statistics are frightening – many teachers will have more pupils in a class from broken homes than from stable families – and thinking about the impact on the kids involved leaves me feeling very sad. I can think of nothing worse for an eight-, nine- or ten-year-old in particular than suddenly having your home torn apart because your parents break up. In my experience, when that happens, discipline often goes out of the window.

I don't know why that is – you would need to ask a psychologist – but I suppose the youngsters perhaps feel deserted and maybe betrayed. Undoubtedly they will be very unhappy, and who can blame them? Children need a mother and a father, and being forced into the position where they have to go with one or the other, or even to choose between their parents, must be horrific. The foundations and order of their lives are turned upside-down. And when their parents are at loggerheads as well, the atmosphere must be terrible.

Sport has an immense contribution to make to the all-round education of our children. In addition to providing essential recreation and an outlet for their physical energies, it has much to teach them from a social point of view. The discipline inherent in any sport encourages good behavioural patterns – every game has rules, and you must abide by them. It also builds team spirit, the 'all for one, one for all' ethos that develops a sense of responsibility towards one's fellow human beings.

I've seen sport transform the lives of some difficult kids. There was a boy at one school where I taught who was, not to put too fine a point on it, a real pest. He was always getting into trouble, larking around and distracting his class-mates. When this lad was selected for the school's rugby B team, those of us who had had to teach him had no great faith that he would be the slightest use to them because of his problem with indiscipline. To our astonishment, almost overnight, he became a completely different child. He had been put in a situation he'd never experienced before, a position that commanded and demanded respect, and he rose to the challenge. I think rugby provided a release for some of his frustrations and a form of discipline that he was able to accept and enjoy. It was a remarkable turnaround.

Another thing that worries me is the alarming number of school sports grounds that have been sold off for development. Once a school loses that kind of facility, it is unlikely ever to replace it. Again, it is the pupils who suffer.

In my view, physical education remains a vital part of the school curriculum. There are those who suggest that it should not be regarded as a subject worthy of study and practice within school hours. I disagree completely with that. Surely now – when children are getting less exercise in the course of their daily lives than ever before, spending increasing amounts of time in front of the television set or computer screen and more often than not being driven to and from school – the need to encourage fitness at an early stage has never been greater?

Lack of exercise is a major factor in the growing problem of obesity, caused by our sedentary lifestyles and compounded by a poor diet based on addictive high-fat foods loaded with salt and sugar. Years ago, pupils burned off excess fat in a variety of ways. Those fortunate enough to be at schools with large playing fields benefited from hockey, rugby, soccer, cricket or athletics. Others, like me and my pals, played in our back yards. We got all the exercise we needed kicking a ball about outside and just having fun running around, and we also walked or cycled everywhere rather than being taken around by car.

I feel so sorry for the gargantuan youngsters you see coming out of sweet shops nowadays, stuffing God knows what down their throats. Such bloated bodies will be uncomfortable to lug around throughout their lives and will in all likelihood lead to premature heart problems and related illnesses. The trouble is, once you become fat it is hard to lose the excess weight and regain your fitness. Parents have a responsibility to ensure that their children eat sensibly and take regular exercise, and if they need help with this, there are plenty of places where they can go for advice. If the illnesses associated with bad diet, such as diabetes and certain cancers, continue to proliferate, healthcare costs will soar, which is presumably why governments are starting to get concerned about the matter. We are storing up huge difficulties for ourselves in the future, and someone is going to have to pick up the bill.

All these problems need to be addressed by society as a whole, yet looking at the teaching profession now from the outside in, it seems to me that far too much of the burden of dealing with the consequences of the general ills of contemporary life is falling on to the shoulders of teachers. They appear to have become almost de facto parents and guidance counsellors for our children. As well as trying to inculcate the need for discipline, standards of decency and a tolerance and consideration of others, they must be aware of the delicate situations affecting many of their pupils in their home lives and treat them accordingly, not necessarily with kid gloves, but with sensitivity. Then they are attempting to instil within children's minds the importance of a good diet and exercise. And when all that has been done, they can perhaps get down to teaching the children history, English, mathematics, geography, computer studies and so on. It is an enormous job.

What disturbs me most about this state of affairs is that society frequently fails to support those in the teaching profession. We are close to asking the impossible of our teachers. We want them to be bright, well educated, highly qualified and understanding. They must be able to handle all aspects of teaching, a task that has become unreasonably multi-layered. They deserve our backing for all they do and yet too often it seems they do not get it. As a society we have become increasingly critical. We want to challenge everything and everyone. There is nothing wrong with that up to a point, but if we simply undermine those charged with the education of future generations without making a positive contribution, we are taking a big risk in terms of the kind of young people we will see emerging from the system.

Too many teachers have already decided that too much is being asked of them and are walking away, disillusioned by the demands of the job and the lack of support from governments that ought to be making their lives easier, not harder. Too many parents are failing their children. If our teachers start to fail them as well, where on earth will we be?

There is no simple answer. Like other problems of twenty-first-century life, it has not arisen overnight and will not be solved instantly. All I can say is that I believe it is essential that teachers are given every assistance and opportunity to perform their role to the very best of their ability. The task is tough enough as it is.

CHAPTER 7
COMMENTARY

TEACHING DURING THE WEEK AND COMMENTATING FOR the BBC at weekends seemed to me the ideal set-up. It was a combination I loved. Wherever I commentated, whatever the match, and whether it was for radio or, later, television, I think I always experienced the same anxiety I'd felt the first time I broadcast live, followed by a surge of adrenaline as I began. Beforehand I was very tense. I listened to the feed down my earphones from the studio, hearing bits and pieces. When I became aware that the previous programme was coming to an end, I knew I was almost there. I was always quaking until I heard the producer say, 'Cue Bill,' but as soon as I opened my mouth, I was fine.

After a while I didn't worry about the nerves, because of something Peter Thomson, the very experienced head of outside broadcasts for the BBC in Scotland, said to me. 'The day you don't feel kind of nervous, pack it in.' It was excellent advice. It is a fact that if you are too laid back, you make mistakes. I always used to say to Bette, 'Well, gorgeous, if I make a botch of it, it's not for want of preparation and trying to do the best I can.'

The BBC were wonderful to work for, and the people there were very helpful and supportive. I was following in the footsteps of some celebrated men, such as the talented cricket commentator John Arlott. His voice got a real grip on you, and I thought he was tremendous. He was also one of the first broadcasters to bring a regional accent to the airwaves. I could imagine a small boy sitting close to the wireless somewhere in the outback of Australia, listening to that rich Hampshire burr, unmistakable to cricket-lovers all over the world, welcoming listeners to the BBC World Service to Lord's for the opening day of the Ashes Test match between England and Australia. I was mindful of the wide audience to whom I, too, was now broadcasting, and that enhanced the pleasure of it for me.

In those days, the BBC was seen almost as a kind of upholder of moral values like decency, and honour, and standards of behaviour and language. Today it is not perhaps viewed in quite the same light, but I do not believe it has lost its prestigious position altogether. In other parts of the world, especially, it still commands huge respect. Certainly, I was chuffed to bits to be working for the corporation. You were more than aware of the standing in which it was held and you felt your contributions had to reflect that position of eminence. Poor, shoddy, ill-prepared work was just not appropriate as far as I was concerned.

Yet when I first started, some of my fellow commentators didn't seem to do much in the way of preparation at all. They just went along to the match and commentated. But I have always been the type who likes to dig up information, and I felt I should try to accumulate as many facts about a fixture and the players taking part as I could. I wanted to fill in the little gaps, maybe tickle the interest of the listener with an appropriate statistic here or there. Very early on, I learned an invaluable trick from one of Britain's most esteemed broadcasters of all time, the late Richard Dimbleby.

The great man was in Hawick to record an edition of a BBC programme called *Down Your Way*, which became very well known and went on for years. The programme would visit a different town or city each week and interview local people, telling the story of the area. As the junior reporter I was sent along to interview Dimbleby about it for the *Hawick Express*. When I got to his room at the local hotel where he was staying, a remarkable sight greeted me. There was paper strewn all over the place, sheets and sheets crammed full of handwritten information. I asked him what on earth they were all for.

'Well, working on radio always requires a great deal of homework, and this is some of my back-up material for the broadcast,' he told me. 'Of course, I wouldn't expect to use much more than five per cent of it, but you must be properly prepared.'

Sounds familiar? Yes, that was how my crib sheet was born. Dimbleby was a good man, very fair with juniors like myself, and generous with his time and advice. Later, when I thought about what he had said, I decided that I should follow his example with my radio commentaries. And so my crib sheet became a part of my arsenal for every single rugby match I ever covered. I didn't quite know what to put in and what to leave out, so I worked on a simple philosophy. Put it all down, and whatever you don't need, don't use. It was as straightforward as that.

At the top of the sheet, I would write down anything I felt would be useful for my introduction to the match. So, for example, when Wales played Scotland at Cardiff on 6 April 2002, my sheet started with the words: 'There are six changes from the Welsh side who leaked 50 points to England. Rhys Williams and Mark Taylor restored, Stephen Jones to call the shots in a pacy back division with a potentially brilliant back 3. Barry Williams, Ian Gough and Colin Charvis to pep up the pack, the forthright Charvis succeeding the injured Scott Quinnell as captain.'

Then below that, I would add all my detailed information on every player in the team. So for that game, alongside the name of Kevin Morgan, the Swansea full-back, I wrote: '1st cap v USA 97; 10th in row; Try v France in this Six Nations; Most Promising Player in Wales 96–7; Youth (caps 8) in 96; Youth Slam 96; Wales Under-18 Triple Jump. Swansea, Pontypridd. 5T [tries] = R97 [Romania], I98 [Ireland], Jpn01 [Japan] (2), F02 [France].

Next to Wales's no. 14, Rhys Williams, I listed his age and physical measurements in a left-hand column. Then I added: 'Spectacular solo try v Italy on 2 March; 1st = FB v I00 [first cap at full-back against Ireland in 2000] week after 20th birthday; 3T = USA00, Tonga01, It02 [the tries he had scored to date in years 2000, 2001 and 2002].

I would go through each squad, setting down all these details for every one of the twenty-two players (the selected fifteen and seven reserves). Then would come the more general information I might need at some stage, for example, notes on how the record of each country would stand if they won.

'So Wales repeat their success over Scotland of two years ago and record their 58th win in this series to 45 by Scotland.' Or: 'Wales therefore compensate in part for that 50-point concession to England a fortnight ago to finish up in mid-table in this Six Nations match. Scotland, meanwhile, finished 2nd from bottom.'

If Scotland were to win the game, I would be able to say: 'So Scotland record their 10th win over Wales at Cardiff and their 46th win in the series to 57 by Wales. It means that Scotland finish in mid-table of this Six Nations Championship whereas Wales are second from the bottom with 4pts from 5G.'

Below this would come all the statistics I might require to cover a game authoritatively: each side's highest points win, biggest defeat, most tries in a match, leading try-scorer of all time, leading points-scorer of all time and most conversions, penalty goals and dropped goals in a game.

These statistics, of course, related only to the two nations playing in that day's match. Supposing one of the players, say Stephen Jones, the Welsh outside half, or Gregor Townsend, the Scottish fly-half, went on a scoring rampage? Suppose one of the teams began to threaten the world record for most tries in a single game, or penalties converted or points accrued in total in one international? I would sound stupid if I did not have the relevant figures to hand, all up to date, with which to inform the viewers of the situation. For example, if Jones scored forty-four points that afternoon, would it be a world record? The answer would be found in a small line in the middle of my chart. There, I could see the category, 'Intl. Rec.', and beside it the line, '45 S. Culhane (NZ) v Jpn95 (T, 20C),' which told me that the All Black Simon Culhane held the world Test match record with forty-five points, and how they were made up.

You had to prepare for every eventuality when you did your homework. What if the referee was injured during the match and had to be replaced? Someone tuning in to watch at home might wonder how many times that had happened, and when the last occasion had been. I saw it as my job to keep every viewer fully informed, and to have every nugget of inform-ation at my fingertips, ready for use if required. International referees are so fit nowadays that it is very rare for them to be replaced during a game. But accidents can happen of course, and if the referee at Cardiff had needed to come off for any reason that day in April 2002, I would have looked at another small section on my chart and read: 'Refs off. R.W. Gilliland F v W65 (B. Marie); R. Calmet E v W70 (R.F. Johnston); K. Pattinson F v S73 (F. Palmade).'

Then there were all the results and scorers from the previous eight matches between the two countries, and after that, the International Championship records that might be broken by an individual or team.

Finally, I had a miscellany of other information that might be useful. At my disposal that afternoon were the answers to the following, if I needed them. When did Wales last play at the old Cardiff Arms Park? When was the Millennium Stadium opened and what was the first match played there? What did it offer in terms of hospitality suites? Was it the tallest building in Cardiff and what were the measurements of its sliding roof? ('220 metres long, 15 metres high.') Which matches were played there in the 1999 World Cup? What was the story behind the pitch? ('Unique grass rotation scheme to counter lack of sunlight. Each section of pitch can be rotated.')

In short, I could offer enlightenment on just about every single aspect of the game or its location that might come up during the course of my commentary. I never considered it excessive because you never knew exactly which item of information you might need. You might go twenty-five years watching rugby and never see a player break Simon Culhane's then world record for the most points scored in an international, but equally it could go at any time.

I did everything I possibly could to avoid being caught out, but I nearly was once, at Twickenham, during England's game against Australia in 1982, when a very well-built young lady by the name of Erica Roe came sprinting on to the field at half-time, minus the top half of her clothing. I'm glad I wasn't down with the England boys, standing in a huddle on the pitch discussing the first half while they sucked their oranges. Apparently, England scrum-half Steve Smith interrupted captain Bill Beaumont's pep talk by saying, 'Er, excuse me, Bill, but there's a bird coming down the field with your backside on her chest.' I think that was just about the end of the England half-time team talk!

At the time, I was doing a wrap-up report on the first-half action, talking into the microphone and looking down at my notes, oblivious of what was going on. I did hear some shouting and cheering, but I had long since become accustomed to not allowing myself to be distracted by that. Then I heard the voice of our producer, Bill Taylor, in my earphones. 'Keep going, keep talking. We'll pan in so tight we're not showing it.' It was BBC policy not to show streakers. But I still had no idea what the 'it' was as I finished my piece and handed over to Gareth Edwards, my fellow commentator that day. At last I looked up and saw this young lady with what you might term an ample bosom bouncing down the field. 'I can still see the look on your face now,' Gareth told me years later. Poor Gareth. He could hear the jokes and laughter all around him and by then knew what all the fuss was about, but he had to remain deadpan serious and straight in what he said, and afterwards I felt guilty about having handed over to him at that precise moment. I can assure him that it was completely unintentional.

I got on fine with Gareth. I had a deep respect for him as a player, and I was very happy with him as a co-commentator, too. I always felt we had quite a good arrangement and I enjoyed working with him. He added to the detail you could give the viewer and I thought he did so very well. Somehow, though, I never got the feeling that he was himself totally comfortable working in television. No matter: he was fair, to the point and had good strong opinions, but I don't know that we benefited fully from his vast knowledge of the game at every level.

I also liked working alongside Bill Beaumont, who took up the co-commentating role after his retirement from the game. Bill had great experience as a captain and that came over in his views, which were quite forthright. He was a pleasure to be with, a very likeable man, and we helped each other. Another former player I was teamed with in the commentary box in Scotland was Andy Irvine, one of the most exciting players our country has ever produced. He was technically astute in his comments, perhaps more than any of the others. He had a gift for imparting information to the viewers that was stunning in its detail, but at the same time managing never to blind them with science. I always felt that people at home must have been absorbing a lot from his knowledge of the game. I have no doubt Andy could have developed into the BBC's number one analyser/ co-commentator, covering matches in England as well as Scotland, but I don't think the idea of trekking south most Saturdays was his idea of fun.

Going further back, I worked for a time with Sammy Walker, the British Lions captain of 1938, who had taken up commentary as a summariser. Mostly that was for radio, though I think we did join forces for a handful of the early televised games. Sammy took his job very seriously indeed and always did his homework. Whenever there was a match in which Ireland were involved, Sammy would be there. He was very down to earth, another likeable fellow, and he always managed to provide a lot of background information for the listeners.

As for my homework, putting together all the material for my prompt sheet took a great deal of time and effort. I would start filling in my sheet on a Monday evening when I got home from school, and work on it every night, trawling through all the reference books I kept in my office at home for little snippets and updating my statistics. By Thursday morning, when I would be packing my bag for Cardiff, Paris, Dublin or London, it would be complete.

In the weeks before an international or club game I would also try to go and watch the players train whenever I could. Tuesday and Thursday evenings would often find me standing on a muddy touchline somewhere in the Borders, probably with the rain pouring down the back of my neck, making notes about a player or two. Then I'd go away to a corner of the field under my umbrella (if I had one) and do a practice commentary to myself, to get used to their names. The locals were used to it, but at international training sessions I'm sure some folk must have thought I'd got a screw loose, standing out there all alone, talking to myself. But I found it was the best way to get to know players and familiarise myself with the way they looked and played.

Before the Scotland–France match in 1976 at Murrayfield, I would have said something like this: 'And Fouroux clears to Romeu; now it's Sangalli on the break, Bertranne is alongside him and here comes Droitecourt into the line from full-back. There may be a chance here for Gourdon on the outside.' Or if it were a Welsh match I was about to cover, I would perhaps have been visualising a Gerald Davies try. 'Phil Bennett skips inside, he finds J.J. Williams . . . now he has real pace. Ray Gravell is alongside him to add the power, and now it's Gerald Davies going for the corner . . .'

There was a very good reason why I took such meticulous care to get it all right: if I ever identified a player incorrectly in my commentary, I was really, really angry with myself. Identification is the number one priority for commentators, and in my view it is almost always inexcusable to get it wrong. If you were a forward who had just driven the opposing pack backwards for ten yards and the commentator said it was someone else, you'd be furious. If that commentator was me, I'd be furious enough with myself for both of us.

It was important to be able to link a name or face instantaneously to a number, because often all you could make out in a pile of bodies on the pitch was a shirt number. It was no good hesitating to check which body was in which jersey, because by the time you had done that the play might have gone on past another four men. I learned a great way of memorising players' numbers from Raymond Glendenning, the old horse racing commentator. I made a pack of fifteen cards, like playing cards, each with a player's name on one side and his number on the other. I practised with these in the run-up to a match. You would get into a rhythm and soon, with just a flick of a card, your brain would be instantly connecting name with number. Raymond used to have cards matching owners' colours to horses' names, and I thought it was a great idea. It was probably the best memory aid I ever discovered for commentating.

As for the names themselves, it was one thing getting them off pat with players from English-speaking countries, quite another when it came to some of the tongue-twisters from other parts of the world. Especially when the Hong Kong Sevens appeared on the rugby map. Now, I've always loved sevens. Indeed, the abbreviated version of the fifteen-man game is part of our local heritage, for it was invented by a Borders butcher, Ned Haig, from Melrose. The Melrose Sevens remains one of the highlights of the Scottish season, and the major fixture on the club sevens circuit. Every spring people flock in their thousands to Melrose for one of the great days in rugby football in Scotland. We've seen some marvellous, magical players there over the years, including the Frenchmen Denis Charvet, Jean-Pierre Rives and Serge Blanco, Australians David Campese and Mark Ella, and the best runners from the game in England, New Zealand and South Africa.

It is a long way from the Scottish Borders to Hong Kong, but one day back in the 1970s, it was announced that a sevens tournament was to be held there. I was sceptical about the kind of rugby that would be played in Hong Kong. It was still a British colony, and I thought it would be a joke event, a few expats, all desperately out of condition, coming together to have a bit of fun. Nothing wrong in that, of course, it was just not something in which I would have had any involvement. But of course the Hong Kong Sevens turned out to be anything but a joke. As the tournament grew in stature year by year most of the world's greatest players took part.

One year I was invited to go out and cover it. It presented alarming difficulties for a commentator. There were wee fellows there with names that I had not imagined even in my nightmares. As the big Fijians warmed up, I was scrutinising the team sheet I had been handed, trying to work out whether a player with a name like Naucabalavu was a wing or hooker, whether an Oolambalabucabuca was really a centre or a converted prop, and whether an Alifereti Doviverata played flanker, full-back or hooker. Really, it was an absolute horror story trying to identify those boys, not to mention pronounce their names.

And of course, throughout the 1980s and 1990s, until the New Zealanders began to get their act together and challenge them, the Fijians reigned supreme, interrupted only occasionally by an Australian Seven. I became a little like the harassed mums you see on the touchline at local rugby clubs on Sundays, watching their children playing in a mini-rugby festival. They want their boys' team to do well but they don't want it all to go on for ever. And what happens? Little Jimmy or wee Scott and his chums keep winning, progressing further and further in the tournament, and they are there for the duration.

The Fijians were wonderful to watch, but those names! Dear, oh dear. And then there were countries like Korea, China, Japan and Malaysia. In each case I had to make sure I had a pretty good idea of who was who. Believe me, it was one of the toughest commentary jobs I have ever undertaken. Unlike the other spectators, you can't go just for a bit of fun – it isn't a holiday, it's a working trip – and you do not want to let your standards slip just because you happen to be commenting on groups of players you have never seen before. So you have to prepare as best you can, study the practice sessions and attempt to remember names and faces, but in those circumstances it is easier said than done. The sevens game is so fast, and the Fijians such brilliant exponents of it, that sometimes you'd find they had scored a try, taken the conversion and restarted the game almost before you'd got your tongue round all the names of those involved.

I went to the Hong Kong Sevens three or four times in all and it was always an extraordinarily well-run tournament. The quality of the rugby on display was amazing. If only it hadn't been for those names . . .

One visit, in 1991, coincided with our fortieth wedding anniversary, so Bette, Linda and Janie came out to Hong Kong with me to celebrate the occasion. We stayed at the Hilton Hotel, then managed by James Smith, a fellow Scot, who was to become a great friend. He was a wonderful host and always looked after me very well. Nothing was too much trouble for him. I remember that year we had dinner there after the tournament ended before dashing to the airport to catch the plane home. But there was one important thing to do before we left. There was a band playing Glenn Miller music in the hotel, and Bette absolutely insisted on a dance or two before we left. I think it made her holiday.

At home, usually the most complicated names I encountered were those of French players. They were nothing like as much of a problem as Fijian ones, but some of them could be tricky all the same. I never saw much French club rugby, but obviously I used to commentate a lot on the French international matches, especially those in Paris.

There I came up against Bertranne, Ondarts, Dospital, Imbernon, Condom (you had to be careful with that one), Droitecourt, Dubertrand, Codorniou and Camberabero. I'm just glad I wasn't around the commentary box in 1931 when the wily French fielded a player rejoicing in the name of Henri Empereur-Buisson from Béziers. He only won two caps. Perhaps even the selectors couldn't get their tongues round that more than twice.

The internationals in France were great occasions, especially the games at the old Parc des Princes, which was more like a bullring than a rugby ground for atmosphere. I loved that. France had some marvellous players down the years, and not only did you have to pay attention to their names but you had to keep a sharp eye out for what they might do next. You could be following the ball down the back line and suddenly, as if they'd pulled a rabbit from a conjuror's hat, the movement would switch and continue in the opposite direction.

When I began commentating, it was always on the radio, of course, which required an altogether different kind of technique from television work. You had to paint a vivid picture for the listener, remembering to describe things that you would take as read with a television audience, which could see for itself what was happening. I liked to try to give as much visual information as possible. I wanted to offer plenty of facts as well, but not at the expense of reporting the live action. No one wanted to hear about so-and-so's family background and how many tries he had scored last year when the roar of the crowd in the background was telling them something important must be happening on the pitch. So you always had to put the live action first, in terms of description, and fit in the statistical information to enhance the story.

When I had a few years' experience of radio work under my belt, the BBC bosses asked me if I would like to become Scottish BBC television commentator. Frankly, I was not sure. I suspected that commentating on television would be an entirely different discipline from radio commentary, which by then I had got used to. In the end, I did accept the job offer, but my fears proved more than justified. It took me a while to appreciate that you didn't have to supply all the details because the viewer could see a lot for himself. A glaring point, I know, but nonetheless it was a difficult adjustment to make. I was accustomed to picking up the microphone and simply talking until someone told me to stop, so I had to learn to adapt. When I first started doing television work, I received a number of letters from viewers telling me in no uncertain terms that I talked too much and too often stated the obvious. That gave me food for thought.

But the staff at the BBC were very enthusiastic and so keen to make the best use of whatever talent you had. People like Leo Hunter in Glasgow encouraged me all the way and was full of praise for the style of commentating I had brought to television with me. I don't think I ever had a problem with the BBC about anything, and I don't imagine many people can say that of an organisation for which they worked for fifty years.

They never batted an eyelid, for example, about arranging first-class rail travel for me. Mind you, that was not something I'd have dreamed of asking for had it not been for the intervention of a colleague, one of the most wonderful, caring, kind men I ever met: Rex Alston. No, I still couldn't believe my luck that I was actually being paid to go to rugby matches at all.

My expenses were drawn not from London but from the Scottish end of the BBC, and they were notoriously careful about how they spent their pennies. So when Rex and I were sent to Paris in the early 1950s to report on a France–Scotland Five Nations Championship fixture, I was booked on the train down to London and then the London–Paris boat train third class all the way. I didn't mind at all. As I sat on the train, clattering and bumping through the beautiful winter sunshine heading south into England, I felt like the most fortunate man alive to be going to Paris to watch Scotland play a rugby international – and at someone else's expense, too.

I changed trains in London, and settled myself in my carriage. As the Kent countryside rushed by, who should pop his head round the door but Rex Alston. 'My dear chap,' he said, in that familiar, beautifully articulate voice, 'what on earth are you doing travelling *third* class? You work for the BBC! You must travel *first* class with me.'

The compartment was full of people and I was rather embarrassed, but Rex insisted, so I got down my luggage and repaired to the first-class compartment, and I must admit, the view looked even better from there. After that, I was always booked first class.

Now, I'm not one to waste money, not even someone else's, but there is no doubt that when you are going to be working on a journey, it is a great help to travel first class by rail, or, when flying, business or first class. It is generally quieter in those sections, and far more conducive to getting your work done.

I considered it a great honour to be working alongside some of the great talents of broadcasting. Of course, many of my former BBC colleagues have retired now – Julian Wilson from horse racing, David Coleman from athletics and Harry Carpenter from boxing, to name but three – and inevitably others, like rugby's Peter West and Peter Bromley from racing, have passed away. These were men who set an exemplary standard and I felt privileged to be a part of the same organisation as them, and in some cases contributing to the same programmes.

Richie Benaud has been a sheer delight for more years than he probably cares to remember. Would a Lord's Test match be the same without his dulcet tones, not to mention his shrewd eye for the game? And I love hearing Peter Alliss commentate on golf, with his little tales and asides. For me, Peter has been the best of the bunch because he always seems so laid back. The great thing about Peter is that he has done it all himself. He has won championships and played in foul conditions on links courses where you could hardly stand up straight, never mind hit a ball properly. He's suffered the agony of those missed putts. All this comes out in his commentaries. I think his lovely, gentle sense of humour also helps to make his commentaries so special. In a technical sense, Peter has always been the consummate pro-fessional. His pacing is always astute. He never seems to be rushed: he does it in his own time and he always seems able to reach for a wee story to enhance the moment or explain an incident. You never get the feeling that he is ramming information down your throat. The secret of his success has been that he makes his viewers very comfortable indeed, yet as he is speaking they are learning things about the game all the time.

I once played golf with Peter in Scotland and saw at first hand his extraordinary abilities on the course. At one hole, our line to the green was blocked by a row of tall trees and the conventional route, certainly the one I was used to, would have been laying up short and playing a long iron with your second shot. Not for Peter. He pulled a driver out of his bag, wiggled it about a bit in his hands and said, half-amusedly, 'I think we'll have a little draw of the ball here.' The next thing I knew, he had smashed the ball hard off the tee and it was climbing into the sky like a jet aircraft on take-off. Then it started to turn sharp left. I rubbed my eyes in amazement as the ball curled away around the trees and went bouncing on down the fairway, finishing right in the middle. It left him the easiest of short irons to the green. It was all done in such a matter-of-fact manner that I was left dumbfounded. I just wish I'd been able to play the game like that. It was an amazing shot.

I think the BBC still does a hugely professional job with its sports commentaries. The new generation of commentators and summarisers has developed a very attractive style of presentation, both in terms of what they have to say and in what they choose to draw attention to. In rugby they offer a variety of interesting information that is most helpful to the viewer. At the same time they convey a sense of occasion. Clearly they are enthusiasts themselves and are lifted by events on the field, which I find very positive.

One big change is that today's commentators give the viewers much more explanation as to why a penalty was given or another type of decision made. That is a reflection of the fact that there are more casual observers watching rugby now who won't be familiar with the finer points of the laws, and it enhances their enjoyment of a game, I'm sure, to have some light thrown on the referee's actions. I don't know whether I could claim to have started that process, but from the beginning it was always my aim to help my audience understand what was happening. My rugby background was invaluable in that regard. I was always up to speed with the laws because I refereed myself, my schoolboy matches, of course, and some junior games too. And as a schoolmaster, I had to attend every meeting of the Scottish Border Referees' Society, which kept me informed as to how referees were thinking. All that came in very handy when I was commentating, and I was usually pretty clear what was going on and why.

From the point of view of the pictures, televised sports coverage has improved vastly over the years as technology has advanced. Now it can show you things you would never be able to see from a seat at the ground. The close-up replays in rugby are hugely revealing: there can be no denying that those wicked, devious hands are pushing the ball back on the ground when they shouldn't be. There are few miscreants who can escape the intrusive glare of the cameras, and anyone contemplating some illegal move is well advised to think again. I think that has to be a good thing for the game. For any game, in fact. People watch sport for the skills demonstrated by the participants, not to see foul play. In a game like rugby you will always get the odd punch thrown in frustration, but dangerous misdeeds are thankfully becoming fewer, and there is no doubt that television has made a major contribution to that development.

What role BBC Sport will play in the future of British sports broadcasting, with so many more companies in the field who all want to be in on the presentation of leading sports events, is hard to predict. The main factor is, of course, finance. Whether the BBC can match the amount of money being put on the table by other broadcasters is open to question. The BBC, still beholden to the licence-payer, are limited in their resources while their competitors seem to have endless amounts of cash to throw about. It would be sad if the BBC were to be pushed aside in many more of the top events. They have always set the benchmark for broadcasting in Britain, not to say the world, and in my time, I took a real pride in being their rugby commentator. I felt the BBC represented the epitome of broadcasting, and that status was underpinned by countless outstanding professionals who all did their bit to build the reputation of the corporation around the globe. I salute each and every one of them. When I was commentating, I can hardly think of a single moment when I was not reliant on someone else's support, and my faith in the production teams was not misplaced: they were always calm, collected, confident and efficient. I might, for instance, start talking about some big fellow in the Ireland or Scotland team who hailed from a certain club and, lo and behold, almost before I had got the name out, the producer would have directed one of the cameras for a close-up of the player I was speaking about. I regarded that as real professionalism.

The unrivalled quality of the BBC's work was one

of the main reasons I didn't want to go to ITV. Others, like Des Lynam, a great professional TV man, did of course make the switch, but there are a lot of folk who reckon he has never been at his best on the commercial channel. Maybe the reason for that is the much tighter time schedule under which ITV Sport inevitably operates, with its frequent breaks for advertisements. On the BBC, Des was able to make his own pace. I thought he was remarkable for the way he just sauntered through a programme. He never seemed to worry, and invariably had time to slip in a little joke or pithy comment that entertained the viewers. His relaxed style also created confidence in the studio and in turn helped his studio guests to relax. It is apparent that on ITV he has been under keener pressure, and there seem to be fewer quips and asides as a result. Whether that is a fair assessment I don't know, but it has been my impression and others have shared it.

Whether the high standards of sports coverage that we, as viewers, continue to enjoy from the BBC are echoed in its general programming is open to argument. There are those who say they have slipped. Perhaps that is simply a reflection of what is happening in society as a whole: after all, it would be hard for a broadcasting organisation not to be influenced by trends in everyday life. However, I am inclined to agree with its critics to some degree. Sometimes you see or hear things on television that make your jaw drop. I am not one for the foul language used in many programmes, for example. To my mind, 99 per cent of it is completely unnecessary, and no more than a manifestation of people's declining grasp of vocabulary. There are plenty of words that can be called upon to express frustration, anger, momentary fury or any other emotion, and I do not like sitting there listening to strings of expletives. When that occurs, I usually switch off, and I suspect a lot of other folk do the same. Having said that, the BBC still offers a lot of excellent programmes. With a little more leisure time on my hands since my retirement, I love watching television, especially films and political discussions, as well as sport, naturally.

Having been on the other side of the screen myself, I appreciate the difficulties faced by those at the microphone. There is a lot going on in your earphones, and you need to give thought to what you say and how you present it, both in general and on the spur of the moment. For instance, how far should a commentator go in criticising players? Having played rugby myself, I was only too aware that things happen in an instant and that you can sometimes be under extreme pressure for a few seconds. Perhaps someone tackles you a bit late, and without thinking about it, you swing an arm back at them. I knew what it felt like to be held back and obstructed when you didn't have the ball. So I was reluctant to denounce every player for doing that sort of thing.

I remember once being ticked off while playing for Hawick for clapping my hands down on a fellow's shoulder prior to putting him on the floor. Afterwards I forgot all about it. A day or two later, I was walking along the street in Hawick when there was a knock on the window of the National Bank of Scotland. A finger beckoned me to go inside. There stood R.L. Scott, president of the Scottish Rugby Union, no less, who was a big shot in the bank. I thought I was going to get a pat on the back for my performance the previous Saturday, but I couldn't have been more wrong. I was led into the area where all the tellers sat and then into Mr Scott's office, where he told me sternly that I had brought my hands firmly down on to an opponent's shoulders when tackling him.

'Billy, dinnae do it. They don't like it,' I was told. 'Tackle by the legs.'

Hawick Rugby Club has always been renowned as

a very dedicated outfit. Their teams played hard but at the same time the club committee men had clear ideas about what was permissible and what was not. The discipline was very strong.

One part of television work I never did very much of was interviewing. I was never keen on it: I always felt uneasy standing next to someone and just firing off a lot of questions without a sheet of notes in front of me. I didn't relish the prospect of interviewing anyone with no chance to prepare my questions. I didn't mind people interviewing me, but for some reason I was never comfortable the other way round. I had to do it on some occasions, but it was never with great happiness in my heart. Looking back, I feel perhaps I should have volunteered to do more and developed a technique that suited me, but it's not a major regret. Commentary was always my natural habitat.

Someone once asked me how I would like to be remembered as a commentator. I said: 'Just for being fair.' Of course, when Scotland played I wanted them to win, and I was delighted whenever they scored a try. But I made it a policy always to see the other team's good points. I am sure this attitude came from my father, who taught me always to listen to and have respect for the other fellow's point of view. My goal was always to provide a commentary so balanced that no one who didn't know me would be able to tell that I secretly hoped for a Scotland victory. I felt I had an obligation to be fair to everyone, and if England scored a lovely try against Scotland, I should say so, and give credit where it was due. There is nothing worse than a commentator who is blatantly biased. You are not being professional, or doing your job properly, if you are guilty of that.

Besides, I had an affection for all the sides I saw, in different ways. If you loved rugby, you couldn't fail to savour the performance of the great New Zealand, Australia and England teams. Then there was Ireland, with their harum-scarum way of doing things. You were never quite sure what would happen next. And of course I was as thrilled as anyone when the magnificent Welsh sides of the 1970s got going. Sometimes they seemed almost invincible and the quality of rugby they stitched together could be breathtaking. The French were a delight for their innovation. Few can play rugby like the French when they are in the mood. So although I am sure there was never any doubt in viewers' minds that I was a Scot and proud of it, I hope they realised that I also revelled in the rugby other teams played. Fine play on the field simply swept my commentary along, no matter which team produced it. I am pleased that at no stage of my career did anyone ever say to me, 'You were biased'. On the contrary, people have been kind enough to compliment me on being fair. I think my father would have been very proud of that.

Still, you can't please everyone all the time, and not even all the Scots have been pleased with everything I have said. After Scotland played France in the final international ever staged at Parc des Princes in Paris in 1995, I had a complaint from one Scotland player. For all the world, it looked before the game as though France were going to record another home success. The Scots had not won in the French capital for an extraordinary twenty-six years. When France led 21–17 in virtually the last minute, it seemed a familiar tale to tell. But then the inventive Gregor Townsend weaved a wee bit of magic, confused the French defence and managed to offload the ball from the tackle into the arms of the onrushing Gavin Hastings, Scotland's full-back and captain. Gavin had some way to go to reach the French line, but he did so with a flourish. He picked the ball up, put it down for the conversion attempt and banged it through the posts. Moments later, the final whistle blew and Scotland had won a famous victory, 23–21.

I can't remember the exact words I used as Gavin made his run for the goal-line, but I do remember what he said to me when I saw him a week or two later. 'I listened to your commentary on that game and you sounded surprised I could run thirty yards!' Well, Gavin wasn't the quickest full-back in the world by any stretch of the imagination, but he was one of the bravest, and there was no question how thrilled I was by that try of his. It was a real moment of drama.

But in my time I've also had a Scotland international almost on his knees in gratitude to me. Scotland found themselves in Bucharest to play Romania on a couple of occasions in the 1980s, and during one of these I had a desperate call from one of the players soon after they'd arrived, early in the week of the game. I was due to fly over on the Thursday for the match. 'Bill, could you please bring some food with you? There's virtually none out here and the boys are starving,' pleaded the voice at the other end of the line. So it was that W.P. McLaren checked in for the flight at Edinburgh Airport loaded down with tins of corned beef. Well, if it was good enough for our boys during the Second World War, I reckoned it would sustain the Scottish lads behind the Iron Curtain. It must have done

ABOVE LEFT: *Jack Manchester, captain of the New Zealand All Blacks, who came to Hawick in 1935. I'll never forget the size of his hands, like great buckets!* (© Empics)

ABOVE RIGHT: *The brilliant Jack Kyle, playing for Ireland against England in the 1957 Five Nations Championship. Jack was a genius, one of the best I ever saw.* (© Empics)

RIGHT: *Australian David Campese, in action against Ireland, during the 1991 World Cup quarter final. I loved Aussie coach Bob Dwyer's quote on 'Campo': 'Bill, I make it a policy of mine never to interfere with bloody genius.'* (© Colorsport)

ABOVE LEFT: *One of Hawick's finest, centre threequarter Jim Renwick, who played for Scotland and the 1980 British Lions.*
(© Colorsport)

ABOVE RIGHT: *Derek White, David Sole and Finlay Calder in Five Nations action, Scotland v England, Murrayfield 1988. Scotland 6, England 9.*
(© Colorsport)

LEFT: *A famous day in Scottish rugby history and one I'll never forget. Chris Gray, David Sole and Finlay Calder celebrate Scotland's 1990 Grand Slam triumph over England by 13 points to 7 at Murrayfield.*
(© Getty Images)

RIGHT: *Another Hawick man, wing Tony Stanger, scores Scotland's fifth and last try in their 38–10 demolition of Ireland at Murrayfield, in the 1997 Five Nations Championship.* (©Empics)

BELOW LEFT: *The brilliant Irish centre Brian O'Driscoll, one of the best I've ever seen, eludes the Scottish defence in the 2003 Six Nations Championship match at Murrayfield. It was an unhappy day for my country, Scotland losing 36–6.*
(© Colorsport)

BELOW RIGHT: *Genius lights up any stage and the brilliant C.M.H. (Mike) Gibson, here in action for the British Lions, was one of the finest ever seen in the British Isles.* (© Colorsport)

LEFT: *Three of the reasons for Wales's dominance of British rugby in the 1970s: from left, Gerald Davies, Gareth Edwards and Barry John.* (© Offside/L'Equipe)

RIGHT: *J.P.R. Williams on the charge for Wales, against France at the old Stade Colombes stadium in Paris.* (© Offside/L'Equipe)

BELOW: *Gareth Edwards, in typically powerful fashion, stretches to score, despite the attentions of Jim Renwick and Andy Irvine in a Wales v Scotland Five Nations match.* (© Colorsport)

LEFT: *A lot of Scots never wanted to see an Englishman lift the World Cup. But if Scotland couldn't win it, I was pleased Martin Johnson's men succeeded in Australia in 2003. It gave northern hemisphere rugby a real boost.* (© Colorspost)

BELOW: *The 1989 British Lions front row: from left, David Young, Brian Moore and David Sole. The Lions came from behind to win the Test series against Australia 2–1.* (© Colorsport)

BELOW: *The flying Welsh wing J.J. Williams, a wonderfully exciting runner, beats French centre Roland Bertranne into the corner to touchdown at Cardiff Arms Park, March 1976. Wales's 19–13 win earned them the Grand Slam for the fifth time.* (© Empics)

RIGHT: *Few could match the sublime running skills, vision and touch of French full-back Serge Blanco.*
(© Offside/Mark Leech)

BELOW: *French scrum half and captain Jacques Fouroux, the man they called 'Le Petit Napoléon', breaks through the Welsh defence, during the 1976 Five Nations match at Cardiff. France lost a titanic contest 19–13.*
(© Empics).

LEFT: *Rugby World Cup 1995, in South Africa, saw the arrival of a phenomenon, All Blacks wing Jonah Lomu. He destroyed England and is seen here beating Springbok full-back Andre Joubert. What a size, what a player!* (© Colorsport)

RIGHT: *New Zealand looked odds-on certainties to win that World Cup but here is Springbok fly half Joel Stransky dropping the late goal which won the Cup for South Africa (15–12 after extra time) and sent an entire nation into celebration. Who can forget, too, Nelson Mandela's presence at the award ceremony?* (© Colorsport)

LEFT: *The neat, articulate and assured Michael Lynagh of Australia.* (© Offside/Mark Leech)

ABOVE: *I spent all week filling in one of these sheets prior to every international on which I commentated. A tip from the late Richard Dimbleby gave me the idea and I never covered a major match without doing my research. As someone once said, 'Fail to prepare, prepare to fail.'*

BELOW: *Farewell, then. I can tell you, there was a right old lump in my throat when I heard the crowd applauding me at my final Five Nations commentary game, Wales v Scotland, at the Millennium Stadium, Cardiff, 2002.* (© PA Photos)

the trick, too, for they won the match that weekend.

Although I'm very much a home bird, and always have been, a certain amount of travelling went with the territory of a sports commentator. But I tried always to get back home to Hawick on a Saturday night. I would usually leave home on a Thursday once my school duties were completed. At one time I caught the evening train for London which came through Hawick, just as I had done as a wee boy with my father. But the wonderful little local line from the Borders up to Edinburgh, which I had taken on my first visit to the Scottish capital all those years ago, closed down in the 1960s, so after that I had to go by car. When air travel became routine it was a great help to me, as it meant I could be in Paris, say, by late Thursday night, whereas before I had never managed to arrive much before Friday morning at the very earliest.

Once the match was over on the Saturday afternoon, I was away. If I ever offended anyone in my haste to get to my car, or to an airport or station, I am sorry. The fact is I have never been a great one for socialising, and I just wanted to get home as soon as I could. In Dublin once, I had two police outriders escorting me out to the airport, clearing the way for the chauffeur-driven car in which I was travelling. I felt like royalty behind that little lot, I can tell you!

Twickenham was no problem because I could get out to Heathrow easily from there to catch the shuttle flight back up to Edinburgh on a Saturday night. Paris and Dublin, likewise. Cardiff used to be a bit more difficult because you couldn't get a direct flight from there to Edinburgh. So I would have a car waiting outside the ground to take me to Cardiff station, and try to catch the first London train out. At Reading I'd get out and transfer into another car, which would rush me to Heathrow for the Edinburgh shuttle. I'd usually land in Edinburgh about 8.30 or 9 pm and I'd be home, with my feet up, having a nice cup of tea, by about 10.15 or 10.30. Then I'd sleep in my own bed, which suited me perfectly.

The travelling sounds complicated, perhaps, and sometimes it was. But as I said, I am a home bird, and I never had the slightest desire to live anywhere but Hawick. I am a family man, too. My wife and daughters have always been the focal point of my life. Bette and I were proud to have two such beautiful daughters and I loved spending time with them as they grew up.

They were great characters, and quite competitive. I remember some family tennis matches, Bette and me against Linda and Janie. They soon disintegrated because if the girls started losing, they would blame each other, leaving Bette and me surveying the scene on the other side of the net in complete bemusement as this private war raged between our opponents. Afterwards it would be about an hour before they would speak to each other, but then things gradually returned to normal.

Like all parents, we had our difficult times, of course. One year the girls – having developed their tennis skills somewhat – were chosen to play for the school team in a match up in Edinburgh. But as luck would have it, this game fell on the weekend of the Common Riding in Hawick, the social occasion of the year in the town. Neither of them wanted to go to Edinburgh. Indeed, they were adamant.

Nobody understands better than I do the importance of the Common Riding, but I tried to explain to them that they couldn't just let their teammates down. The school tennis team was a unit, and they would be failing all of the other players if they didn't go. In the end they went, albeit with extremely grumpy expressions on their faces. They lost, but I was proud of them for making the effort to participate. In later years, both Linda and Janie told me I'd been right to persuade them to go, which meant a lot to me.

And we had a few problems when they were teenagers! We all went on holiday to Venice once. They walked around the city wearing just what you would expect any sensible, sober Scottish lassies to wear in a country where the menfolk have a reputation for excessive libido. Mini skirts, I was told they were. Whatever they were, they were like a red rag to a bull. The whistles were deafening as we walked by, and I'm sure they weren't directed at me. When any passing young men stared at our girls' legs, I tried to stare back just as hard, conveying the message that they should keep their hands to themselves. But Linda and Janie just lapped up the attention.

Memories of watching our daughters grow are precious, and I wonder how many of them I might have missed had I spent less time at home. Frankly, after a rugby match, it just meant more to me to get back and see the three loveliest ladies I ever knew than to sit at an official rugby dinner half the night, listening to a lot of speeches and watching people drink too much. It was as simple as that. Don't get me wrong, I'm no killjoy. People can do whatever brings them pleasure, and good luck to them. But for me, there was never much appeal in trawling around a series of bars for most of the evening, or dressing up in a dinner suit and tucking into a gargantuan, six-course dinner. It just wasn't my scene.

I had the balancing act of home, school and commentating down to a fine art. But then one day the BBC presented me with an awful dilemma. They asked me to go in for a meeting, and when I got there and we sat down, they told me they wanted me to become a full-time commentator, reporting on rugby during the winter and tennis and athletics in the summer months. I would be going all over the world, covering British Lions tours to Australia, New Zealand and South Africa every four years, and to Paris, London, Dublin and Cardiff as usual for the Five Nations Championship each winter, and goodness knows where in the summer. The Olympics, for example, would be part of my brief. A dream job? Well, to some, perhaps, and initially it sounded great to me, too. First-class travel all the way, the finest food and luxury accommodation. How could I turn that down?

Easily, once I thought about it. When I discussed it with Bette I realised just how much I would have to sacrifice to do such a job. There was no way she would be able to come with me – she had plenty on her plate at home – and that meant I would be travelling around, staying in an endless succession of hotels all on my own. My master plan of getting home each Saturday night would be in tatters. I would be away Saturday nights, Sunday nights, Monday nights – most nights, in fact. There was another big problem. I would have to move down south, to somewhere within striking distance of London. If you were needed in the London studio a lot, you could hardly commute there from Hawick the whole time. The job would mean a major upheaval in my life and the lives of everyone in my family.

There would doubtless have been a very handsome salary, but I have no idea how handsome, because we never got as far as discussing money. Once I'd thought it through, I knew there was no way I wanted to make all those sacrifices. Even if the BBC insisted, and told me the only way I could keep my existing rugby commentating job was to take a full-time position, then I would, with much sadness, have had to let that go. I just knew I could never tear myself away from my lovely home, and all the people I had grown up among, and with whom I felt such a close allegiance.

Happily, the BBC accepted my decision, and allowed me to continue my commentary work part-time. It was a great relief, as it would have been a terrible blow if they hadn't. I think they realised that my reasons were genuine and just how strong my ties to Hawick were.

So I still had my commentating, teaching and time with my family, and I was as happy as a sandboy. My routine for international weekends rarely varied. On a Friday morning, wherever I was, I would watch whichever of the two teams playing the next day was less familiar to me in training, memorising faces and names in conjunction with the jersey numbers their owners would be wearing. In the afternoon, I would try to see the other team, but if that was not possible, I would stay in my hotel room and study my chart and my numbered cards with the players' names on them, turning them over again and again until I was razor-sharp.

I always tried to get a good night's sleep on the Friday in the hotel. Over the years I must have turned down countless invitations to dinners and other events on the Friday before an international, but I couldn't allow myself to be distracted. So I would have a relatively early supper, usually on my own, and then retire to my room to spend another two or three hours going over my papers and immersing myself in every detail of the forthcoming game, storing away little snippets of information in the back of my brain.

On Saturday mornings, I liked to have a good breakfast because I wasn't one for eating just before a match commentary: it didn't sit well with those butterflies! I might have a short chat about the match with any supporters who were around at the hotel, and then return to my room for my final preparations. These entailed turning over my numbered cards in rapid succession, putting names to jerseys, to check just how many details I had retained. By this time I would expect to be 100 per cent correct with every identification, and I'd be pretty upset with myself if I got anything wrong. There wasn't much more time for rehearsal, so I had to get it right.

Well before kick-off time, at least half an hour or so, I liked to be up in the commentary box, comfortably settled with all my papers spread out around me, secure in the knowledge that I was all set to go. Mind you, some of the commentary boxes were pretty rough and ready, not to say difficult to get into. To reach the old TV gantry at Murrayfield you had to climb up a shaky ladder, clutching your briefcase. I often wondered halfway up it who would do the commentary if I fell off.

The best commentary positions for me were the open-air ones. The TV gantry at Lansdowne Road was in the old stand, but it offered an excellent view.

Twickenham was the same, and at the top of the old Murrayfield stand – once you eventually got there – the panorama was superb. You were not protected from the elements, of course, but I felt that being able to feel how cold it was, or trying to keep dry in driving rain, was part of the experience. The conditions and the general atmosphere were a factor in the game to both players and crowd, after all, and I wanted to share their perception of the afternoon as fully as possible. Sitting in a heated room enclosed by doors, walls and glass, you felt a little cut off from the proceedings. The commentary box at the Parc des Princes in Paris was one of those and for me it spoiled the experience somewhat because the atmosphere outside in the stands was always fantastic.

All I needed in any box was a basic chair and a bench on which I could lay out all my things. I know that some TV commentators, like Murray Walker, preferred standing up to commentate, but that wasn't my style. I liked to sit down and be comfortable. For over ten years, I had a very able assistant called Alan McCredie, a schoolteacher from Hawick. As a referee of school and junior matches, he was ideal for the job, and he loved doing it. Alan would come with me into the box and keep notes of all the important features of the match, the principal incidents and of course all the scores. At the end he would hand me three big foolscap sheets of paper, and, based on his notes, I could do a two-and-a-half or three-minute report to the BBC Scotland studio. I always trusted Alan's judgement.

When it was all over, when I finally got home on a Saturday night, that was it. I always slept like a log. I was not one to lie awake, twisting and turning, replaying the commentary in my own mind and fretting about how I could have done it differently. I was probably too worn out by all the travelling and rushing to catch plane, train or car after the game. Whatever the reason, I never had a problem getting to sleep. What I did do, though, was watch the game when it was shown again on the Sunday, identifying little faults, and making a note of them for the next time. It is amazing how much you can miss in a fast-moving game, and as the game improved in recent years and became a great spectacle, you really had to be on your toes.

Mostly, I'm pleased to say, I was quite happy with what I'd done. I loved the job, but that love would have soured if ever I felt I'd failed to live up to the exacting standards I set myself. So I tried always to keep my feet on the ground.

I'd have been delighted to have continued as a

commentator indefinitely, provided I was up to it – you got a good fee and I still have to keep my wife in twin-sets and golf balls – but seriously, the last thing I wanted was to end up making mistake after mistake and becoming an embarrassment to anyone, least of all myself or my family. It was essential to me that I knew I had done a good job. So when I began to feel that I was not quite as sharp as I had been in my earlier days, that my reactions were not quite as quick and accurate player identification seemed slightly more difficult, I knew it was time to go. Things happen very quickly on a rugby field and whereas in the past I had always been able to keep up with whatever happened, I was beginning to find myself struggling a little with the pace. You have no time whatsoever to think. Things happen, bang, bang, bang, you have to get all three names right as the ball goes through different pairs of hands and if you're not quite there with it, you won't be pleased with yourself. As you get older, you simply do not function as quickly as you used to, and you have to recognise and acknowledge that fact. I had always wanted to finish on a high note, and I hope I did that.

Of course, a big part of my life was taken away the day it all ended. It was a hugely important part of my life, but never *the* most important part. My wife and children were always clear winners in that league table.

When I reflect on those fifty years of commentating, I still marvel at how fortunate I was. Fortunate to have been given the opportunity in the first place, fortunate to have met so many fine people and fortunate to have been able to do the job on my terms and to fit it around the rest of my life. Many has been the time, especially since my retirement, that I have sat down at my home in Hawick and remembered the person who made it all happen for me. For the fact is that without John Hood, my old boss on the *Hawick Express*, and his kind thought in writing to the BBC about me, none of it would ever have happened.

CHAPTER 8

INTERNATIONAL RUGBY

WATCHING SCOTLAND PLAY INTERNATIONAL RUGBY HAS been one of the great privileges of my life. Ever since that first occasion when I marched down Princes Street with my dad, my wee hand in his, on my way to Murrayfield for the first time, every occasion when Scotland has played has been special to me. It remains a huge disappointment to me that I never got the chance myself to pull on the famous jersey, listen to the last-minute team talk and run out to play the auld enemy at Murrayfield. I have spent my entire life wishing that I could somehow have played, even just once, for Scotland in a full international. It would have meant more to me than anything else I can think of in a sporting context. When I played in that final trial at our national ground, just entering the dressing room was a thrill in itself. I was awestruck.

But Scottish international rugby today is very different from the Scottish international rugby I first came to love. I was born in 1923, and from then until the outbreak of the Second World War, Scotland played England sixteen times. Of those matches, England won only seven, Scotland eight and there was a draw in 1930. A cliffhanger it was, mind – 0–0 at Twickenham. Compare that sequence of results between the two countries with, say, those from 1987 to 2004, a period which encompasses the first five Rugby World Cups played to date. In those seventeen years, the nineteen matches have produced quite another picture. England won sixteen, one was drawn and Scotland have taken just two, in 1990 and 2000. Now, I'm old enough and wily enough to know that statistics can be used selectively to prove any point. But I don't think there is any getting away from the fact that these figures indicate a major shift in rugby power within the northern hemisphere in favour of England.

It is a situation that has been exacerbated by the arrival of the professional era. England is a country with a massive population, huge playing numbers and vast financial resources for things like sponsorship and player support. To set England alongside Scotland in those areas is plain daft. Yet that is what is happening. The English juggernaut is rolling right over the likes of Scotland at international level, and I do not see any prospect of it being halted. Indeed, it has been suggested that the problem will get even worse. I don't know about that, but I do know that Scottish international rugby faces some significant difficulties in the years to come.

Some have also maintained that Scotland have fallen behind because they do not have the infrastructure. Well, if by infrastructure they mean the kind of resources enjoyed by England, then they are right. But in truth, it is not so much a matter of Scotland degenerating as of England stepping so far forward. The Scottish system is still thriving. We have our three provincial sides in Glasgow, Edinburgh and the Borders, and they play matches between themselves and within the Celtic League, so there is a competitive structure reaching right down to the grass roots. Furthermore, our clubs continue to play with fervour and ambition. But I think everybody acknowledges that we do not have sufficient reserve strength. We do not have the number of class players countries like England and France can call upon. So, Scotland has to make the very best of what it has, and I don't think that is happening at present. Certainly, it is a struggle for the national side to keep its head above water, as results such as the 20–14 defeat by Italy in Rome in the 2004 Six Nations Championship underlined.

England have advanced much more effectively and significantly in these last ten or fifteen years than probably any other country. So when the remaining five nations take them on, they do so as underdogs. If you get the better of England, as Ireland did at Twickenham in 2004, you have done very well. Even France have had to look to their laurels to match them. The Six Nations is in danger of becoming a two-horse race. It was gratifying to see Ireland taking the Triple Crown in 2004 because the tournament needed that kind of upset. However, the big problem for all the other northern hemisphere countries is to consistently mount a meaningful challenge to the reigning World Champions. English resources are so strong that it appears they will continue to dominate. Furthermore, the coaching system seems to be good and Sir Clive Woodward, who seems to me to be a sharp boy and pretty forthright, has created a very impressive squad. Some of their results recently have made me sit up and marvel at their ability to go forty points up in a Six Nations Championship game, often without very much trouble at all. And I don't mean against weaker opponents like Italy, either.

Take the 2003 Grand Slam game against Ireland. Ireland had not won a Grand Slam since 1948, and hopes were high that in Dublin England could be toppled. Both teams were unbeaten in the Championship, so it was a classic winner-takes-all shoot-out. But look what happened. England didn't just win, they slaughtered Ireland, 42–6. In a match between unbeaten teams for the Grand Slam, that was a simply incredible result. I believe there will be serious long-term consequences to this English dominance.

England's overwhelming superiority over Scotland in recent years may dissuade people in future from continuing to pay high prices for tickets to go to Murrayfield for England games. People get sick of seeing their team not only losing but suffering heavy defeats. There was a much better display by Scotland in the 2004 Six Nations Championship, even though England ran out comfortable winners in the end by 35–13, and there was great support for the Scots that day, but it is the general trend that is worrying.

Supporters and players from the grass-roots game are finding it hard enough as it is to afford a visit to Murrayfield for an international these days. On top of the £50 or £60 a stand ticket costs, there is travel to Edinburgh and back to take into account, plus a meal and other general expenditure. At a conservative estimate, you are looking at over £100 a head for a match, which is a lot of money. If a father wants to take his son, he will have to find in excess of £200. And internationals are no longer the rare events they used to be. The expanding fixture list puts an extra financial burden on supporters, and may force them to stay away from some games. I would not want to see internationals priced out of the pockets of the vast body of rugby followers, the kind of people who support their clubs day in, day out. They should be able to have a good day out at Edinburgh watching their national side at a reasonable cost.

I think the authorities need to be very careful not to kill the goose that lays the golden egg. Sometimes I feel there are an awful lot of spectators at Murrayfield nowadays, perhaps from the corporate world, who don't know much about rugby. They are there because it is an occasion, and to maintain the integrity of that occasion we really need the regular, genuine supporters to be in the majority at our national ground. They are the people who know what is going on and why, and who will lead the way in good behaviour and in showing the right kind of encouragement to the team. If you lose too many of these supporters, then you are leaving your game open to the influence of folk who do not understand rugby, or all the good habits and customs that have always been at its core. Customs like not abusing the referee, not booing while a player is lining up a kick at goal, not shouting out offensive remarks, not cheering when a member of the opposition is injured.

If the superiority of England and France continues in the years to come, perhaps another major competition will emerge pitting them against New Zealand, Australia and South Africa. Although South Africa have been struggling a bit recently, they have significant numbers and resources in their vast country, and they were good enough to beat Ireland (twice) and Wales in summer 2004. As a nation they expect success and don't take kindly to anything less. Whether this will happen only time will tell.

It is my fervent wish that the Six Nations Championship should survive and maintain the position it has always held in rugby people's hearts. It is the traditional centrepiece of the season and has always generated huge interest, notwithstanding the recent monopolies of England and France. The Championship is much envied in the southern hemisphere. Until they began their Tri-Nations competition, they had nothing remotely similar, and even that is not really comparable: the European tournament sees thousands of supporters travelling to our various capital cities for the big games, whereas in the southern hemisphere, following your team in the Tri-Nations is not an option for most rugby fans – the time and distances involved would be as daunting as the cost.

In my view the Six Nations is vital to the health of rugby in the northern hemisphere. If its status were undermined – if, for example, England and France did become part of an annual world competition and began to field something less than their best team in the Six Nations – or worse still, if the Championship were to be abandoned altogether, the impact on the game in this part of the world would be severe.

I wonder whether one day the Championship might be expanded to include eight or nine countries. If some of the lesser lights – Romania in particular – can advance sufficiently, then it could happen. The difficulty, as ever, will be financial. If your game is a minority sport, which rugby clearly is in a country like Romania, then it will be a big struggle.

I suspect that Scotland will have to be altogether more realistic in the future about the standards we can attain. What we will perhaps have to accept is that there will be comparatively few occasions when a Scotland team can win the coveted Grand Slam. In an ideal world, honours would be spread more evenly, but all is not necessarily gloom and doom. A powerful England do at least provide a benchmark against which the rest can measure themselves in world terms. England have always been the target of the Celtic countries and I think that state of affairs will not only continue but intensify. Anyone who knocks over England will have every reason to be delighted, and will gain themselves tremendous kudos with everybody else in the rugby world.

Scotland and Ireland, in particular, have a rugby history of long periods of hunger in which nothing happens, punctuated by a sudden great success, bringing a short burst of joy to the whole nation. That was the case when Scotland last won the Grand Slam, in 1990, and the entire country rejoiced. The euphoria was probably all the greater because it was obvious even then that the event was becoming rather unusual. Perhaps we will have to acknowledge that it will always be like that.

Scotland's comparative shortage of players has persuaded the national side to reach out to other countries for qualified candidates. In Scotland's 2003 World Cup squad, for example, we had players born in Sittingbourne and Chatham in Kent, St Helens in

Lancashire, London, Newcastle-upon-Tyne, Wagga Wagga, Sydney, Brisbane and Melbourne in Australia, and Wellington and Auckland in New Zealand. That is a fair spread of the net but they were all eligible under various rules. The connections of some players have been tenuous and of course, like most Scots, I wish that our team could be made up only of players born and bred in Scotland. Yet it wouldn't be right to preclude players born in England and elsewhere of Scottish parents and whose loyalty to Scotland is genuine. Although we wouldn't want the team to be too dependent on southern hemisphere players with Scottish allegiance, it should be acknowledged that a number of them have made impressive contributions to our cause. Sean Lineen, from New Zealand, was a huge success in the ranks of Boroughmuir FP in Edinburgh as well as claiming twenty-nine Scottish caps. He made his home in our country and even when he retired from playing, he gave valuable service with his coaching. Brendan Laney, also from the southern hemisphere, has already gained nineteen caps and 141 international points. There was some resentment when Laney was first capped because he seemed to have come from nowhere, but in time he, too, made his mark on the Scottish scene.

However, the sight of fellows jetting in and picking up a cap straight away does concern me. I am sure I speak for all true Scots when I say that I never, ever want to see our national jersey devalued in any way. To cheapen it for short-term success is quite simply not an option in my book, and it seems to me that if you invite anyone with the slightest family link to switch hemispheres and represent Scotland, you are in danger of doing exactly that.

I feel that Scottish rugby will have failed if it does not provide a proper incentive for its own young players to reach international status. I can just imagine how disappointing it must be for a young player on the verge of a cap who feels that he has bust a gut to get himself fit, learn as much as possible about the game and improve his techniques, only to see some guy from New Zealand, South Africa or Australia suddenly come over and get in ahead of him. There can be nothing more dispiriting for a player than that. So I am a great advocate of making sure that the qualification is secure and that every potential international has a watertight entitlement to wear the blue jersey. If any player is a marginal candidate in any sense, then in my view he should not be selected. History and tradition mean a lot to us, and I do not believe there is anything wrong in that.

Certainly no Scotland national team, whatever the make-up of its personnel, should ever lack the essential qualities of team spirit, camaraderie and sheer will to win. Added to tactical awareness, those qualities can take you a very long way indeed, as Scotland sides have shown in the past.

There were some class boys in our 1984 Grand Slam-winning side, no question. But probably the key ingredient was their team spirit, epitomised by the captain, Jim Aitken. There was a strong element of 'We're Scots and this is Scotland' in the deciding match against France at Murrayfield. Jim Calder's try that day seemed to sum up the spirit and intense will to win within the team.

It was the same in 1990, when Scotland met England in that classic Grand Slam decider at Murrayfield. Bette came with me to watch England train on the Friday afternoon. They were big, strong, fast, gifted, switched on, very much together and they showed a high level of skill. It was a quite superb training session, and it impressed everyone. At the end I said to Bette, 'I don't know if Scotland can beat that lot.'

Yet on the day, partly thanks to the Murrayfield crowd and partly because of a clever tactical approach to the game, Scotland won. Just twenty-four hours earlier, I really could not imagine Scotland beating that England side, but they did it. Perhaps there was one quality they had that I had under-estimated: a strong heart. That match proved that it *can* be done, even if such moments of glory do become increasingly rare for Scotland teams in the Six Nations Championship.

That day was one of the highlights of my career from a purely nationalistic point of view. It was a phenomenal achievement, and I was a proud man in more ways than one up in the commentary box, watching one of the young lads I had helped coach at school, Tony Stanger, score early in the second half the crucial try that broke England. Scotland's rugged defence went on to hold out in the last twenty minutes against all that England could throw at them. I had to make extra sure that there was not so much as a hint of bias in my commentary at any stage of the match that day, which was no easy task.

I suspect that I would find it hard to be either impartial or positive about some of the things that go on in the international game today. I worry about the sheer physicality of the play and the number of actions that carry the possibility of serious injury. As a schoolmaster who helped teach lads about rugby, and perhaps even introduced some of them to the sport, I felt responsible for ensuring through my teaching methods that they could carry on playing it as adults and enjoy it in a healthy, sporting sense as well as a competitive one. Certainly it was a game in which there were plenty of knocks and bruises – that comes with the territory. But exposing players to the risk of severe, long-term injury, especially through dangerous or foul play, is unacceptable.

Professionalism has by its very nature imposed several requirements. Players have to be fitter, stronger and faster. Rugby has always been a tough, physical contest, and there is nothing wrong with that. Withstanding an orthodox tackle, in which your opponent grabs you round the hips and slides down your legs to bring you down, in the way all schoolboys are taught, is hard enough; having someone batter you at a hundred miles an hour with the express intention of knocking you backwards if at all possible is something else altogether. When you see a fellow dip his shoulder and blast an opponent back, or hurl himself into the pile of bodies at the point of breakdown, it is a wonder there are not more injuries. If you are the guy standing beside the ruck and you are hit by an opponent flying flat out, and his head strikes you on the body, it is a hell of a shock to the system. Who could pretend that such high-impact collisions are either necessary or safe? Then there is this business of grabbing a player by the legs and pulling them up in the air so that he crashes down on his back, shoulder or neck: the so-called 'spear tackle'. To me, that is without question a dangerous tackle, and referees should be coming down hard on it. Thankfully, it doesn't happen too often, but I have seen one or two of them go unpunished recently.

The very fact that we now talk of 'big hits' and 'high-impact collisions' rather than tackles is an acknowledgement that rugby has become more physical than we would ideally want it to be. I don't think this can continue to increase – we are probably seeing it reach its peak now – but it is already frighteningly close to the limit, and it is imperative that the law-makers and referees make certain that players are protected. I would like to see these excessive challenges eliminated from the game. International rugby is demanding enough as it is, and it would be better off without them.

You could argue that the onus should be on coaches to stamp them out. After all, it is up to a coach whether he trains his team in a sensible or a reckless way. There is plenty of evidence to suggest that some coaches go over the top. They must encourage their players to go out and give their best, of course, but they should draw the line at dangerous practices. Very often, players go on to the pitch with something other than the spirit of the game on their minds. Seeing some collisions nowadays, I think to myself, 'How did that laddie get up after that?' In a physical game, you cannot prevent players being hard and committed, and it is to the credit of the game that for more than a hundred years, serious injuries have been kept to a minimum. But the game that has been played for more than a hundred years is not the game that is being played today, at least not at international level. This is something entirely different, and it requires different safeguards.

In the end, it is the officials who carry the real burden of responsibility. They are the ones who must frame the laws, and who should be looking at the game and legislating to remove those innovations that have crept into the game and which are plainly hazardous. It is the referees who must enforce that legislation and ensure that players are safe from the odd guy who exceeds the bounds of acceptability.

The decision to let rugby become 'open', in other words professional, has many potentially far-reaching consequences. One is that if this culture of 'big hits' starts to seep down to the lower reaches of the game, it could create all kinds of difficulties. In addition to the danger that many mothers will take a dim view of their sons playing rugby at all, the most obvious is that many referees at junior level may feel the responsibility they must bear has become too great. If a player were to be badly injured, the official in charge of the match might be caught up in all sorts of legal ramifications. We live in an increasingly litigious age and legal challenges arising from sports injuries are bound to become more prevalent. It is different if you are a professional referee taking charge of a match between Australia and England. You will be experienced, and thoroughly trained and prepared to handle a match at that level. You will also be fully insured. Not every junior referee meets these criteria, and he could find himself in a legal minefield if a heavy impact resulted in paralysis or other serious condition. Some referees already have. Others may weigh up the risks and decide that what is, for many, a purely social and unpaid activity on a Saturday afternoon simply isn't worth it. You could hardly blame them. Yet what is the future for rugby if referees turn away from it?

There is no doubt that the demands on the professional player are considerable. To the list of physical requirements we might add a psychological one: whereas once there was a desire to win, it is now a necessity. The stairway to the stars created for the new breed of player leads downwards as well as upwards, so there is an extra pressure on them to produce consistently top-drawer performances. Just trying your best is not enough any more; you must achieve it. There is a subtle but important difference between the two. Rugby is no longer simply their passion but their whole livelihood, and in order to stay on that treadmill of fame and financial reward, they must remain successful.

Bette and I have three rugby-playing grandsons. Our elder daughter, Linda, is married to the Scotland scrum-half of the 1970s, Alan Lawson, who was capped fifteen times, and their two boys have followed in their father's footsteps. They both play at senior level, Gregor for London Scottish and Rory first for Heriot's FP and now as a professional with Edinburgh. Janie's son, James, also plays for Heriot's. Rory enjoys playing professionally, but he also has a degree in business studies to fall back on, having graduated from Edinburgh University in 2003. I believe that is essential. I have reservations about our grandsons making a career of rugby. I admit I worry when I watch them play, because of the increased risk of grave injury. I would also be concerned about their future security and all-round experience of life.

I loved the old amateur game. I loved the routine in which we trained on Tuesday and Thursday evenings, played on a Saturday, and the rest of the week was your own. It was part and parcel of your life, but crucially, it was never the be-all and end-all. In spite of my devotion to the game, I don't think I would have enjoyed training every day, having rugby coming out of my ears. It would have annoyed me that it was preventing me from doing other things. As an amateur sport, it occupied your leisure hours, not your working hours, and I was delighted to give it everything I could in every spare moment. I would even go out and train in the dark on my own. But the constant diet of rugby football, day after day after day, that is the lot of the modern professional player would have been too much even for me. I don't think that rugby, from the playing point of view, was ever meant to be a seven-day-a-week affair.

It is important, I think, to be a well-rounded person with all kinds of interests. Life offers so many opportunities in so many different fields. In the past, by the time fellows had finished playing at the top level, the chances were they had made a lot of contacts in the business world, and if they needed assistance, someone would come along and provide it. But almost everyone combined their rugby with their work anyway, so by the time they hung up their boots, they already had a career that had been developing in parallel with their rugby career, and they were able to concentrate on that. But what will the professional player do when he is thirty-five and has thrown away his boots – and, more pertinently, drawn his last salary cheque – if he has no other qualifications? Where does he go to find employment for the remaining thirty years of his working life? It is the duty of the professional clubs and administrators to plan for the long term and encourage their young professionals to prepare themselves for life after rugby while they are still playing. Many young men live for the present and never worry about what lies ahead. But the fact is that, especially in light of the excessive physicality of the modern game, their career might well end in their next match.

It is very sad that young men today must make a choice between rugby and a career. It cannot be right that if you want to become a doctor, lawyer or veterinary surgeon you cannot play top-class rugby. Both the game and the players are the losers. Some talented people will never reach a level where they can demonstrate their skills, not because they are not good enough, but because the requirements of this new professional sport will not allow them to play in the upper echelons and study at the same time. They will be deprived of the chance to fulfil their potential and rugby will miss out on some class players. Many great names of the past lit up the stage at, for example, Oxford and Cambridge universities before going on to become internationals, British Lions or All Black captains; players of the calibre of Gavin Hastings, Gerald Davies, David Kirk, Mike Gibson, Bleddyn Williams, Wilf Wooller, Onllwyn Brace, M.J.K. Smith. As well as excluding a wealth of potential talent, in this respect professionalism will also create a different type of player in the top ranks of the game – a one-dimensional, identikit type. The rich variety of teams made up of individuals with rounded lives, of hospital consultants, farmers, policemen and builders, are a thing of the past.

As for the game itself, professionalism has ushered in many changes, as well as increased physicality, few of them for the better. Players seem to be becoming unadventurous. Why bother running from sixty metres out when you can kick into the corner, fifteen metres from your opponents' line, and try to steal their line-out throw? 'Eliminate risks' appears to be the prevailing attitude. Part of the reason for this tactic is the unhealthy emphasis coaches everywhere have put on defence. As a result we are seeing defenders stretched across the field from one touch-line to the other, forming a wall that is becoming progressively harder to breach. The attacking side will perhaps have four, five, six or even more recycled possessions in their attempts to break through, but when they cannot succeed, they kick. I fear we have turned our code into a fifteen-man version of rugby league.

Some have even suggested that we should reduce the numbers in union to thirteen in order to free up some space on the field. I believe that would be a terrible admission of failure on the part of rugby union and I don't think it is necessary, either. Even as things stand there are still some magnificent matches, so it is not as if it cannot be done. Generally, though, teams have been too concerned about making a mistake that could be exploited by the opposition. What we need is to see them taking a few more risks. That approach can be coached into them just as easily as greater defensive awareness has been.

The risk element is difficult for some coaches to embrace in an age when winning is paramount, and there are leagues and championship titles at stake. But they should not lose sight of the ethos of rugby: to have a go, to attack, to try to unlock a defence by means of creative thinking, speed and ball skills – the qualities that underpin the whole game. It is important that we remember these as we go forward. I hope that the legislators, too, are monitoring this development and will ensure that we do not drift too far into a negative, ultra-defensive mode. They must keep in mind the need to encourage players to handle the ball rather than kick it, and to provide the kind of framework in which handling the ball is productive and brings some reward. I remember only too well periods when rugby consisted of little more than a succession of kicks, and I can tell you, I have no desire to see them return.

There have been so many occasions when the sparkling accomplishments of the likes of David Campese of Australia, Andy Irvine of Scotland or Phil Bennett or Gerald Davies of Wales have lit up an entire match, producing the special moments, the things that stand out in the memory. Those swashbucklers achieved thrilling feats because they were bold and daring and prepared to take risks. We are perhaps more in need today than ever before of players like them. I loved commentating when they were on the field. Whenever Campese got the ball, he seemed to explode out of nowhere; Bennett, too, came off either foot in the blink of an eye. When rugby is played in that style, with the focus on attack by talented performers, there is no better game in the world for inspiring and delighting untold millions of people. Now, that cannot be a bad thing to say about a simple ball game, can it?

I only hope that rugby continues to look after that kind of player, and to look after itself in the process. There seems to be less and less room in the sport, as in society, for the maverick: the person who bucks the trend, who does the unexpected; the player who, without the instructions of the coach, sees an opportunity opening up and just goes for it. I don't want to see those people ever being squeezed out of the game, or out of society. There should always be a place for the individualist, for the free spirit like the former England adventurer David Duckham. When he took off, blond hair flowing behind him, he could lift a game all by himself.

Of course, if you have the right coach, a man of sufficient gravitas, self-belief and confidence, then you are in safe hands. Clive Woodward seems to be giving sufficient breathing space to Jason Robinson, who has become a key member of the England team since his arrival from rugby league. What an exciting player he is. My goodness, you don't know where those dancing feet are going to take him next. I wouldn't like to be the guy trying to stop him, because he runs rings round the opposition.

I remember once asking Bob Dwyer, the first man to coach Australia to a World Cup triumph, how he ever managed to coach David Campese. 'Bill, I make it a point never to interfere with bloody genius,' was his reply. I loved that. To me it said everything, not only about the sheer unpredictability and wizardry of Campese, but about the genius of the coach, too. A lesser man than Dwyer might have tried to rein in 'Campo', to provide more structure to his game, to make him play more conventionally. And if the player didn't or wouldn't comply, he might have just left him on the sidelines and never harnessed his brilliance for the good of the side. A similar fate has certainly befallen some outstanding talent in the past. Dwyer, thank goodness, had vision. I am sure Campo frequently drove him up the wall, but he never lost sight of the player's dazzling if unorthodox qualities and shrewdly fitted them into his team's approach. It was a mark of Dwyer's coaching skills that he did so, and we should all be grateful to him, because Campo thrilled the world with his genius. He played it off the top of his head, that was what made him so entertaining. His decisions were by no means always correct but he was always worth watching, because when he got the ball, something startling was bound to happen, whether it was a hitch kick, or a crossfield run, or whatever.

In a previous generation, the Ireland fly-half Jack Kyle was another out of the same mould. He was like lightning off the mark. In one game against Scotland, played in rain at Lansdowne Road in 1956, Kyle either kicked the ball or passed it the whole match. He never tried a thing on his own. But finally, with only three minutes left and Scotland leading 10–9, he took a pass from John O'Meara, his scrum-half. From about twenty metres out, he just took off, dancing like a ghost through the Scotland defence and evading everyone to score a superb try and win the game. I remember thinking at the time that Kyle was just about the only player of that era who could have scored a try like that. In those days, it was regarded as almost impossible to score from a set piece. The feeling was, a little as it is now, actually, that you had to create a ruck or maul before you could handle wide. Plus ça change. Today defences are so set that you have to create countless rucks and mauls before you get anywhere. It is like churning butter: a hell of a lot of hard work before you can call the job anywhere near finished.

People have said to me that they don't find the modern game appealing because all you are doing is waiting for someone to miss a tackle. Only when that happens in the back line can one of the threequarters get through and perhaps score. But under the new system of ultra-organised defences, most of the time the ball-carrier is tackled, and then the ball has to be recycled. Time after time after time. I went down to watch Hawick play Stirling County not so long ago. As I watched this ordinary club match unfold, I thought to myself, 'I am bored.' The phases of play were long, drawn-out, tedious and predictable. There was no spark of genius, no unconventional seizing of a chance to break the defences down and galvanise the play. I could not remember ever in all my life being bored at a rugby match before and wishing I was somewhere else. Even in the dullest game, I can usually find something to enjoy, admire or interest me, but I couldn't in this one. It was a development that really worried me. My greatest fear is that I have seen the best years of the sport. I sincerely hope I am wrong. I am not saying we will not appreciate players who are bigger, fitter, faster, stronger and better organised on the field, but it concerns me that I and others like me may not enjoy the way rugby is played in the future.

There are other more minor irritations: the increas-ing use of spoiling tactics, for example, and the changes to the line-outs. Being permitted to hold a lock forward up in the air is a farcical situation that cheapens the whole game. It looks ridiculous to me to see a fellow hanging out to dry until the throw arrives. What a lot of nonsense! You also have players making dummy runs at the line-out, moving from front to back to the middle to try to confuse the opposition. It has all resulted in more untidy line-out work. Occasionally, you do see a game in which there is a real battle for possession and a right good, stirring sight it is, too. It warms the heart of an old 'un like myself, I can tell you. There were some wonderful battles in the old game when you had two big line-out men who could jump vying for the ball. I miss seeing that spectacle on a regular basis.

I make no apologies for saying that I loved the game as it was. Maybe it's just that I am too old to welcome change, but I felt that everybody had their place under the old amateur laws. Players could opt out if they felt like it, and teams were not discouraged by that. Above all, I felt there was a ladder there from bottom to top. You played for your junior club, progressed to a more senior club, then played for your district. Some went to university and played there. Whatever path you took, your talents were on display to the national selectors. If you were picked for a trial, as I was way back in 1947, you were knocking on the door.

I also loved the strong club loyalty. There were people who gave service to one club for twenty or forty years. I do not see that being the case in the future. Above all, I approved of the fact that a guy could play rugby football to the highest level and still do his job. To me, that made sense in every respect. As I said, even the best player in the world is only one bad tackle or one disastrous collision away from the end of his rugby career.

There was talk for years about the game going professional. I was totally against it. I still am. When the announcement was finally made that rugby union was now 'open', what did that mean? That a forty-something player with the Old Rubberduckians Second XV would be finding some cash in his muddy boots before a game? From where and from whom? I think professional players have a lot to offer, and I thoroughly enjoy watching them on television. But they should be playing rugby league, in my view, not rugby union. I do not believe rugby union was ever really suited to professionalism. Was it such a failure the way it was that it had to be completely transformed to secure its future? Did we have to make it professional for it to survive? I don't think so.

But that's 'progress'. You cannot turn back the clock and we are stuck with it. So now we must make sure that we manage this 'new' game well and efficiently, cherishing and nurturing as many of the characteristics and traditions of rugby union as possible. The torch has passed to a new generation, and I believe they can take rugby union forward and look after its customs and history at the same time. It is a big responsibility. If that doesn't happen, in years to come we will end up with a game that is un-recognisable from one which I and millions of others grew up loving, which would be a tragedy.

It has been the greatest of team games, producing wonderful players, astonishing team efforts and quite extraordinary feats of charismatic play. In which other game would lifelong friendships have been forged between guys knocking each other about in rucks and mauls, crashing into each other in scrummages, crunching in against other big lumps who probably hadn't shaved for four days? Fellows have survived all that at every level of the game, from schoolboys up to international level. That is significant, distinctive. There is no doubt that rugby union has brought people together in a way that maybe no other sport has managed. They bash the living daylights out of one another on the field and yet afterwards they're all having a few pints together and singing with their arms around each other. It has offered physical activity, friendship, laughter, fellowship and high endeavour on the field. You can only have warm feelings towards a sport that can create all those things. I consider myself privileged to have been so closely attached to it for such a major part of my life. I would not have had it any other way.

I do not want to give the impression that nothing about the modern game is better than in the past. That would be quite wrong. There have been improvements, chief among them the efforts players have made to better their skills, especially the forwards, both at senior level and in the lower ranks. Their handling abilities have been transformed, not to mention their stamina, running, tackling and covering. At one time, forwards just put their heads down, churned the ball back and then got out of the way. Loose forwards in particular are very much part of the whole strategy of the game nowadays, in both attack and defence. Many of them are even thinking like backs, which has made them a perfect link between the hard, tough guys and the aristocrats behind the scrum. And just about every forward can handle like a threequarter. Not only do they fulfil their traditional role of winning the ball, but they can move it among themselves if it is propitious to do so. It is an enormous compliment to them and to the hard work they have put in.

Yet my overall personal verdict on professionalism is that it has been too high a price to pay. I am uneasy with the concept of businessmen who may have absolutely no knowledge of the sport or feel for its traditions owning major clubs simply because they have the largest chequebook in town. This may appear beneficial in the short term but I see no value in it to the game in the long run. When these men owe no allegiance to the sport and have become involved for purely opportunistic reasons, at the first sign of a rocky patch they might disappear as rapidly as they arrived. Several once-great clubs have been reduced to the ranks of also-rans, and others have all but disappeared entirely.

So we cannot pretend that all is great and glorious with the modern game. A new version of rugby football has been born, complete with new attitudes and ideas, and I suppose that people of my generation must simply accept that, and be content with their memories of the old one. But we can still be thrilled and delighted by some of the skills on display, and heartened that there are still so many outstanding young men playing the game, attracting others to its banner by their famous deeds.

We must trust that the old ideals and standards that have been synonymous with the sport are kept alive. Otherwise we would be entitled to conclude that the game we knew, loved and respected had indeed gone for all time. I certainly hope I never see that happen in the remainder of my lifetime. My greatest wish for rugby's future is that it never will.

CHAPTER 9

CLUB RUGBY IN SCOTLAND

SOMEONE ONCE ASKED ME TO DESCRIBE A TYPICAL MAN of Hawick. I needed to think about that for a moment. My answer was that he is forthright, states his case and does not hold back. He says what he feels and thinks, so you can bank on it being reasonably genuine. He believes in and continues to support the tradition of his town. I have always been and always will be a man of Hawick – indeed, I am extremely proud to have been granted the Freedom of the Town some years ago – and that description certainly goes for me.

History and Hawick go together like ruck and maul. The Saxons lived in these parts around a thousand years ago and called the town Haggawick, which means the settlement hedged around by hills. It is said that St Cuthbert lived for some time on a grassy knowe on the site now occupied by St Mary's Church.

After the fall of the Saxons, the Normans came and erected a wooden tower on Hawick Motte to control the Barony of Hawick. In the thirteenth century, something more substantial was required, so a stone tower was built where the rivers Teviot and Slitrig met. Eventually, the powerful Douglas family came to rule the town and it was Sir James Douglas who granted the town its charter in 1537.

Due to its strategic location so close to the English border, Hawick was a hotbed of war, rumour and intrigue throughout the Middle Ages. There were many battles and skirmishes in the hills nearby, with the English plundering Scottish territory and the Scots fighting back against their ancient foe with raiding parties. The Common Riding ceremonies that continue to this day give a flavour and understanding of what went on in those times.

Wool and its use has been the main local industry since the 1770s, when Baillie John Hardie introduced stocking frames to the town and established a knitwear industry that is still flourishing. More recently tourism has become important. One of the finest attractions of the Borders region is its country-side, and visitors come from all over the world to walk, ride and play golf in this unique landscape. Strolling along the banks of the River Teviot on an early summer's evening is one of life's loveliest pleasures.

There is a football club in Hawick, Hawick Royal Albert, and football does function here, but it has always been a rugby town. Its boys are brought up to believe that the highest pinnacle in sporting achievement is to wear the green jersey. The sport's popularity is partly attributable to Hawick RFC's fine record over the years. They have won the Scottish Championship and Border League more times than any other club and have produced a whole raft of international players.

Although the Greens supplied the Scotland side with backs as well as forwards, it was their forwards for which they were renowned, men like Willie Welsh, Jock Beattie and Jerry Foster. So it was the members of the pack I tended to idolise in my youth, rather than the threequarters. Welsh was one of the all-time great flank forwards. He toured with the British Lions in Australia and New Zealand in 1930, and won twenty-one caps for Scotland between 1927 and 1933. I was awestruck when my father and I bumped into Willie Welsh one day while out on a walk in the Orchard. Beattie, a huge bow-legged lock forward of about 13st 8lbs who was as strong as a horse, was capped twenty-three times between 1929 and 1936. Foster had four caps from 1930 to 1932. They were my heroes.

There were plenty of superb players to be seen at Mansfield Park. I remember my father taking me to see a match against Edinburgh Academicals when I was about eight. We watched a man named G.P.S. Macpherson, who had played for Oxford University – and you didn't do that in those days unless you were special. His ability to weave at full speed was absolutely stunning. He gave us a demonstration of his skill that day, weaving through half the defence and putting them on their backsides before scoring a wonderful try.

Rob Barrie, who played against England in 1936, was a colleague of my father's at Innes Henderson, the Hawick hosiery firm. There was my dad, just chatting away to this legendary Hawick and Scotland wing forward, as they were called in those days. This was before collecting autographs came into vogue, but even if I had wanted to ask him for his autograph I'm not sure I would have managed it. It was all I could do to speak, such was my excitement.

Walter Sutherland, my mother's cousin, had played for Scotland thirteen times on the wing between 1910 and 1914. He was a naturally quick fellow who also ran for Scotland in athletics competitions. Andrew

'Jock' Wemyss, of Gala and Edinburgh Wanderers, who was the great rugby commentator and reporter of my early years and who had himself been capped seven times, in 1914, 1920 and 1922, had played alongside Walter for Scotland against Wales in 1914. He told me once that Walter Sutherland was the best wing he ever saw in all his experience, and believe me, it was a wide experience. When I repeated that to my mother, she burst into tears. For Walter had lost his life in the First World War, tragically, on the last day of the conflict. So the rugby background was already there, deeply embedded in the family, by the time I came along.

Bette, too, was brought up with the Greens. Her father, Rob Hill, was a member of the Hawick team that won the Border Championship in 1923–4, the season I was born. I may have heard the cheer from my pram when Hawick scored the winning try in their vital match against Melrose. Bette's dad had also been in the A side that triumphed in the Hawick League Junior Championship the previous season under the captaincy of W. Scott. There sits that XV today, proud and composed, in an old sepia-tinted photograph on our wall, elegantly dressed in their pristine kit, their clean leather boots neatly laced and their hair neatly slicked, some of them sprouting handlebar moustaches. There are two elderly gentle-men, club officials, in suits with those special detachable collars, their half-hunter watches hanging from chains round their midriffs. Two cups have been reverently placed on the ground before them.

We youngsters couldn't wait for kick-off on Saturdays. Crowds at Mansfield Park averaged around 2,000, with bigger attendances for the best games. It might not sound a lot, but Hawick was a town of only about 14,000 souls then. Now it's closer to 20,000. For a place that size to produce the number of internationals it did was quite exceptional, and testimony to its passion for and dedication to the game. Tradition was always a big part of the scene, and people loved that. For example, Hawick always played Heriot's from Edinburgh on New Year's Day. The local derbies with other strong Border clubs like Gala, Melrose and Kelso all had a special edge to them. They invoked ferocious loyalties and players who took part in them felt as if they were playing for their lives. The intense rivalry between these great old clubs lives on, and long may it continue. The Border League is always keenly contested and it provides the less successful clubs, Langholm, for instance, and to a lesser extent Jedforest and maybe Selkirk, with a chance to have a go at the Hawicks, Melroses and Galas of this world. It is not a case of mutual hatred, but the competitive element is several notches higher in a Border League game than in a match against a city club. In general, the city backs are more skilled, so those encounters tend to be characterised by the Border boys trying to knock them off their pedestal.

Mind you, the local clashes can become a bit heated at times. One referee who was sent down from Edinburgh to take charge of a Borders League match told his pals when he got home: 'It's not a referee they need down there, it's a missionary.'

There is a fierce pride that burns within clubs like Langholm and Jedforest, something for which I have always admired them. They may not have enjoyed quite the success or widespread renown of Melrose, Gala and Hawick, but they are extremely determined. A game between close neighbours will really send the fur flying. Kelso and Jedburgh, home of Jedforest, are only a handful of miles apart so local rivalry is especially strong. Both Jed and Kelso have produced some world-famous players in their time, men like Roy Laidlaw and Gary Armstrong from Jedforest, and Jimmy Graham, Bob Grieve, G.H. Cottington and John Jeffrey of Kelso.

For me, the big rivals to Hawick have always been

Gala, from Galashiels. Matches with them have been real cut-and-thrust affairs in which the desire to win overrode everything else. Nobody was very concerned about entertaining people. Stand down at Mansfield Park when Hawick are playing Gala and you'll hear comments that would make your hair frizz. But after all that blood and thunder between the Greens and the Maroons, as soon as the game is over, everyone will be in the bar, calling cheery greetings to friend and foe alike and generally getting on like a house on fire. Some of the closest personal friendships I've known have been between Hawick and Gala folk.

Hawick and Gala go back over a hundred years. Gala have been in a lower division, but it makes no difference. Whenever they meet Hawick, there is a tremendous upsurge of interest and local support, just as there used to be in Wales when Cardiff met Newport, or Llanelli made the short journey across West Wales to Swansea, their big city rivals. You will get a good three or four thousand at a Hawick–Gala Border League match. Hawick could have played fourteen and lost them all, but come the Gala game, folk will be pouring down the road to the ground.

It's much the same with other Border sides. Hawick versus Melrose is always a dogfight, too.

Like Mansfield Park, the Melrose ground, the Greenyards, is steeped in history. Completely surrounded by hills, rather like Cheltenham in England, it has a beautiful setting. Trees abound, and opposite the main stand is a sloping section giving spectators a good vantage point from which to watch the game. Just behind them, through the trees, sits the local church. I remember the South of Scotland holding the famous 1932 Springboks, led by Benny Osler, to a pointless draw here. There wasn't much that day of what you might call fancy-Dan play, backs strutting their stuff and throwing the ball around the field. It was more of a grim war of attrition in which neither side was prepared to give an inch. It was said later that they could have played until midnight without anyone breaking the deadlock, so tight and determined were the defences on both sides. The South's achievement in holding the Springboks was emphasised when the touring side went on to beat every home nation on that tour: Wales and Ireland both by 8–3, England 7–0 and Scotland 6–3.

The Melrose club have been amazingly successful on very short rations, really. They've had their international players, all right, some of them Scottish legends like David Chisholm and Alex Hastie, as fine a pair of half-backs as I can recall. Then there was

Jim Telfer, one of the great servants of the game in this country, and that elegant, attacking threequarter Keith Robertson, who was club coach in the season 2003–4. Yet overall, Melrose have scrambled along; for a wee town of only about 3,000 folk, they've achieved miracles. But they hold their heads up high, and rightly so.

Some of the battles Hawick had on the ground were legendary. At times there would be eight or nine internationals playing, testimony to the strong junior sections at each club which helped to nurture and bring through their respective local talent. There were a lot of matches in the 1950s and early 1960s, in particular, won by a single score, often a crucial penalty goal. There would be results like 4–3 or 6–5 then, very tight matches that were scraps from first to last, frequently played in pouring rain.

In the depths of winter, the hills would be covered in snow and the slush on the pitch made for conditions even less conducive to attractive rugby. There were plenty of days when the forwards were slithering all over the place and the backs hardly ever got a go at all, beyond the fly-half. I used to love the wheeled scrummage and the dribble in Borders rugby. Wheeling the scrummage was a familiar tactic in Scottish teams from the very early days – in fact I think the Scots were the first to use it. They were great ones for foot rushes, 'dribbling rushes', we called them, and they were certainly hard to stop when performed correctly. At their best, Scottish forwards gave the impression that the ball was tied to their boots, so cleverly were they able to control it. It took a very brave man to fall at their feet and stop a dribbling rush. He'd be 'rummelled up' for sure. It was a way of providing variation, not only in forward play but in testing the opposing back division, because it was quite often the opposition's fly-half or centres who would have to go down on the loose ball and try to stop the forward charge. It could be painful!

Back in the 1920s and 1930s, and even for a spell after the Second World War, the dribbling rush was a big feature of Scottish international play. When I played for Hawick, we spent a great deal of our Thursday night training sessions dribbling up and down the touchline. Tom Wright, who helped the team at Hawick in those days, used to insist we dribbled the ball up and down the terracing side at Mansfield Park. 'Dribble, dribble, dribble!' he would bark, cracking the whip, and woe betide you if you let the ball get too far away from your feet.

First of all, you had to get the wheel of the

scrummage right. It had to be quick so that you could launch your two guys from the back of the scrum with the ball at their feet. The other forwards would rush to join them and take the ball forward. Of course, keeping the ball under control was essential. If you kicked it too far ahead, control was lost. If you let it become trapped in among your feet, the forward rhythm and momentum would go. So it was a real skill, a real part of the game.

It is not seen today partly because wheeled scrums are no longer used. It is thought safer and better to have the ball in your hands. But speaking personally, I would always have a dribbling rush in my repertoire because it is a scare tactic. Given the number of unscrupulous forwards who didn't mind where they put their feet, the backs in the old days would think twice about diving on the loose ball just as a herd of feet came stampeding towards them.

I am puzzled today by the way forwards seem to turn up out on the wing or at centre. To me it says that either they're not doing their job properly up front or the laws need some adjustment. I think only the backs should be out in the back line, to create the scope for classical threequarter play in which the backs can show their skills, measure their passes, assess situations or make breaks. None of those things are really possible if you have the entire back line cluttered up with props, the odd hooker (well, aren't all hookers a bit odd?), a couple of second rows and all manner of back-row men. It's no wonder that often the backs can't get into the game. You don't want great lumps of forwards hanging about in the fly-half position or out on the wing. You want players in those positions who are quick and skilful, players who can use the ball well and entertain the spectators. Surely we see enough grinding forward play in the modern game as it is without having to watch it again when the ball does emerge from the forwards and starts to go down the back line. The donkeys should be doing the donkey work, the backs the clever stuff. Of course, if a lock forward finds himself in the middle of a handling movement, that's great. You hope he will be able to handle as well as the backs and form the link in the movement. But generally speaking, I don't like to see forwards getting in the way in midfield.

The game is so much more technical than it used to be. When I was playing, I remember a Hawick official talking to one of our players about the match that afternoon and the threat posed by a particular opponent. He said, 'What are you going to do if such-and-such happens, and so-and-so gets the ball out wide?' Our man replied simply: 'I'm going to tackle him.' That was it. It all seemed a lot more straightforward then. We just used to go out and play. Yet for all the technical preparation in the modern game, I am not at all sure the intuitive skills are as effective. I don't believe players are able to 'read' a game as well as was once the case. I liked to see players making decisions based on what they saw in front of them during a match, not what someone had said in the dressing room half an hour earlier. The decision-making is not as good, in my view, which may partly explain why threequarter play has not exactly flourished in recent times. I hope it will improve, for there is room for it to do so.

Scotland's city clubs have their own sense of pride and their own strong rivalry, albeit of a different nature to that of the Borders. When Edinburgh meets Glasgow, there is a stack of tradition at stake. These two sides have been playing each other since 1895, and there have been some titanic contests. Although soccer dominates in our two big cities, Celtic and Rangers in Glasgow, Heart of Midlothian and Hibernian in Edinburgh, the rugby fraternities are still very solid. They meet at the beginning of December. I covered that inter-city match as a commentator for a good number of years and it was a fair old duel most of the time.

At least if you play for a city team, you can slip out on a Saturday night after a match and lose yourself. You can't do that in a town like Hawick, Galashiels or Melrose. That ardent local rivalry puts great pressure on players – and not just when they are on the rugby pitch. Your fellow townspeople will tell you straight if you've messed up and lost a game you should have won, or failed in the championship. Boy, will they tell you.

I played for Hawick in the Melrose Sevens once – I suppose it must have been around 1947 – when we were narrowly beaten, only by two points, in the first round by the Edinburgh club Watsonians. I was with George Hook, my fellow prop in the sevens team, later that evening, after we had got back to Hawick, and we were walking along the High Street. It was dark, and there seemed to be nobody about, but we heard the voice unmistakably enough.

'Ee want tae hing up err buits, yow pair,' it said. Roughly translated, that meant, 'You two should retire because you're bloody useless.' There was such disgust in the town that we'd lost in the first round of the Melrose Sevens that people were making comments even as we walked down the street, minding our own business. I've never forgotten that. We never knew who had been addressing us, but it didn't matter. It was just one example of the responsibility placed on the shoulders of everyone who pulls on the hallowed green jersey. It's been that way for well over a hundred years, and I hope it still will be another hundred from now. Because at its root is that deep love of the game, the club and the town.

I've known maybe a hundred or more Hawick people – men, women and children – go down to Mansfield Park at eight o'clock on a Saturday morning armed with shovels to shift two feet of snow off the pitch so that a game could go ahead. I used to cover stories like that for the *Hawick Express* and I was sometimes amazed at their dedication. Will there be as many there doing their bit in ten or fifteen years' time, I wonder? Some might be inclined to say to themselves, 'Well, the players are getting paid to play, why should I go down there and work for nothing?' My optimistic side tells me that people have always given their time to their local clubs and always will; that there will always be those prepared to don their work clothes and get stuck in. I hope my faith in humanity is not misplaced.

In the Borders, youngsters still grow up with the game. The junior clubs still have plenty of players, so it's not as if they're folding or anything like that. In Hawick, there are four junior clubs that feed the senior side and most Border sides have a second XV. In the schools, too, they're still playing rugby.

What has perhaps been eroded is the players' fierce devotion to their local clubs. When money comes into the equation, loyalty can be weakened. The main problem is that paying players is such a drain on a club's resources. So one club will only be able to afford to pay its guys so much while another can stretch to a wee bit more. Many local lads are still determined to play for Hawick or Melrose or Gala or wherever they live, but there is no doubt there is much more switching about nowadays, which I think is a shame. Throughout history, a Gala man would always be a Gala man. Even if he moved to Hawick or Kelso or some other place, he would still be a Gala man through and through.

It is maybe as a consequence of this diluted loyalty to club or region that we are seeing results like the 53–7 hiding the Borders suffered against Edinburgh in the autumn of 2003. That was a disgrace. In my day, people would have dropped their cups of coffee at the thought of the Borders conceding fifty points to anyone, New Zealand included. But now it is seen as just another provincial side. Thankfully, rivalry between the clubs at least remains undiminished.

People still want to support their own town, their own rugby club, while the players want to gravitate to the next stage up, to represent Glasgow, Edinburgh or the Borders, because that is the stepping-stone to international rugby. That is as it should be. We need that layer just below international level as an extra incentive to them. Without it, I don't think Scotland would be able to compete any longer at international level. The club player can see a clear progression if he can reach that rung of the ladder. He can say to himself, 'I am getting there, I'm getting closer to a cap.' It is a good experience for the young players from the Borders because it gives them a sense of the standards in the upper levels. They cannot advance until they can beat Edinburgh or Glasgow before contemplating going to Paris or Twickenham for an international and facing France or England. It is all part of the learning process.

The old national trials used to give players who were knocking on the door of the national side a feel of what it was like to play in a big international stadium. Scotland used to have three, one maybe at a club ground and the other two at Murrayfield. If you got to the final trial, you knew you were on your way and the sense of anticipation was enormous. You also knew you had to play your socks off for eighty minutes to have a hope of earning selection. It certainly made the matches intensive and competitive which, of course, was the whole idea. I liked those big trial matches: there was a sense of anticipation in the air, like at Christmas. They brought a fresh sense of excitement every year, a chance to see what the new crop of players was like and how the national side might measure up for that season's Five Nations Championship. Some 'form horses' would come through and perform as you expected, but there was always the possibility of an upset, of a few lesser-known players seizing their chance and overturning the form.

That is what happened in 1986 when the Reds beat the Blues, supposedly composed of the players most likely to earn national selection, by 41–10. The Reds that day included two remarkably talented young men who were prepared to go out and throw their all into the fray for their team without necessarily trying to impress the selectors with their own individual skills. Gavin and Scott Hastings, the brothers from George Watson's College in Edinburgh, had so dramatic an impact on that trial match that they were both capped for the international against France at Murrayfield. What is more, they handsomely repaid the selectors' faith by helping Scotland to win 18–17, a famous victory in the history of the game in this country in which Gavin kicked six penalty goals.

To play in a trial match is a real test because you have to fit in with the other players, and try to operate as a team man, just as the Hastings brothers did. Naturally, you want to advance your case for a cap, but you cannot function as a lone wolf. That is the secret to it. By contrast, today a Hawick player might play in the Borders provincial side alongside five or six other Hawick men. It isn't exactly a comfort zone, but it will not be as alien an environment for a player as a trial match often used to be.

In the past, when a player from your club was good enough to win a cap, he could bring a wealth of knowledge from the international arena back with him. His experiences from other parts of the world, both on and off the field – all he had learned from training, from conversations with players from other countries and, of course, from the games themselves – could be of immense value.

A perfect example at Hawick was the contribution of Hugh McLeod, who won forty caps for Scotland at prop forward between 1954 and 1962 and toured with the British Lions in 1955 and 1959. Now, Hugh was one of the greatest acquirers of rugby lore the old game ever knew. With the Lions in South Africa and New Zealand, when the other guys were drinking, singing songs and having some fun after matches, Hugh would be sitting in a corner with the local coach, chatting away about his methods and the aspects of the game on which he placed most emphasis. Hugh loved Hawick, and seized every opportunity to gather information that would benefit his club. He would talk to the French about their peeling off the back of the line-out, how they rolled downfield through their forwards, and the New Zealanders would explain to him the technicalities of their rucking game and why they invested such faith in it. Hawick's domination of Scottish rugby for some years was in part due to all the knowledge we gleaned from coaches around the world through Hugh McLeod.

Putting something back into the sport has been the *raison d'être* of countless people in the amateur game who have enjoyed their club careers so much that they have felt the need to do whatever they could to support future generations in the same way that they themselves were supported. Whatever level they played at, on retiring from the game, most players have happily accepted some role at their club, often one that has taken up a considerable amount of their free time. They have served on the committee, or perhaps represented the club at district level, or got involved in coaching one of the junior sides. These former players, and an army of other club members, all serving in an honorary capacity, have formed the bedrock of the sport, going down to their club every Tuesday or Thursday night, every Saturday, and in many cases Sundays too, to clean the kit, wash the dishes, lay the tables . . .

Not only have these men and women underpinned rugby union, but in our towns, and others like them, where local rugby clubs are a part of the community, they are also underpinning that community. Whether they are helping out with teas or weekend trips for the Guides, or taking their turn in organising activities for boys' clubs in their area, or running stalls at their children's school fête, they are contributing to local life. If you take away all the people doing unpaid jobs like these, you weaken the whole structure of the communities that are one of the foundations of society.

I wonder what impact turning rugby into a commercial operation will have on this tradition.

Will we continue to enjoy the freely given support of all these volunteers? If players have been accustomed to being paid for playing, will they be so willing in future to devote years of their spare time to their club for nothing? Or will they have become so used to the concept of payment, of taking from the game, that the idea of giving back becomes obsolete? Will they expect to be paid for being committee men, too? I believe there will still be some ex-players who would serve on committees in an honorary capacity, but others may just walk away from the game once they are not being paid any more. If ever we come to the stage where people will not serve on club committees on a voluntary basis, it will be a sad day.

I know one thing. As sure as night follows day, clubs could not survive without these unpaid workers. The people who stand at the gate taking money, who rush out with first aid when a player is injured, who serve behind the bar, arrange the annual club dinner, and who beg, borrow or steal prizes for the raffle to raise club funds.

Other aspects of rugby culture are being set aside in many countries, as though they are old-fashioned and have no relevance to the modern game. In Wales, we see great clubs with names known the world over like Newport, Swansea, Llanelli and Neath suddenly calling themselves something else. Neath and Swansea, for example, came together to play in the

Celtic League as 'the Ospreys'. In South Africa there are teams called 'the Sharks', 'the Blue Bulls' and 'the Cats'. I'm afraid I get awful testy at this nonsense. If you're the South of Scotland, you're the South of Scotland. If you're Llanelli, you're Llanelli, not the Llanelli Scarlets or the Llanelli Rattlesnakes. Sometimes you are hard pushed to tell where some of these teams are from, which is stupid. What was wrong with Western Province or Northern Transvaal?

Doubtless this is down to the influence of marketing people who have no background in rugby. But why on earth do we need it? In England, though we do have to grit our teeth at the Sale Sharks and the Newcastle Falcons, thankfully most clubs are still using their proper names. Leicester, of course, are also known as the Tigers, but that's a long-established nickname which has been in use for decades. Harlequins have added the initials NEC, the name of their chief sponsor, to their own name, but they're still universally known as Harlequins. At least they are not calling themselves the Mannequins, and Bath haven't suddenly re-emerged as the Romans. To me, silly nicknames just demean the game and weaken its strong identity at club and provincial level. They make a laughing-stock of rugby football.

I hope I never hear Hawick called the Hawick Haggises or Gala being described as the Gala Pies. I don't think anyone would ever get Border clubs to adopt such daft labels. Hawick have been the Greens for 150 years, and I think I'm right in saying that every Hawick member would want them to stay that way, as every Gala member would want Gala to remain the Maroons.

Nothing can stay the same for ever. We must embrace changes to a certain extent in most aspects of life, some pleasant, some painful. But it makes me angry when outsiders ride roughshod over valued traditions. If you don't respect tradition, whether you are a rugby club, an opera house or anything else, you risk losing it, and with it the appeal that attracted people in the first place. Who could then blame newcomers for asking, 'Why is this anything special? There isn't any particular history attached to it, and we don't see what makes it different.'

A club or organisation that retains its core values can offer those who are interested an association which goes back for decades or in some cases a hundred years or more. That, surely, is worth holding on to. So I think the key is not to be in too much of a rush to embrace change for change's sake. Just about everything that is special about rugby could disappear within the course of a few years, leaving us with a game that bears no resemblance to the sport we once knew.

There is one big change brought by professionalism which is very welcome, and that is that players who have gone to rugby league can once again return to their local rugby union clubs. All that many of them ever wanted to do was to put something back where they started out in the game. It is a source of great pleasure to me that we no longer see exclusion around rugby union clubs, and there is no doubt we are better off for that.

There had been a sad postscript to the career of one of my boyhood heroes, Willie Welsh, who was in his time one of the best loose forwards Scotland had ever known and a real artist in the sevens game. In the latter part of his career, he had turned professional and gone to play for a rugby league club in the north of England, but he was still revered in Hawick. As a seventeen-year-old, I was thrilled when a newspaper reporter described me as having shown during a game certain characteristics that brought to mind W.B. Welsh. I cut the piece out of the paper and kept it, I was so chuffed. Willie had been a swashbuckling type of wing forward, with good hands, who got himself all over the field, and to be compared to him made me very proud.

Willie had returned to Hawick when his playing career was over, and some while later, he was invited down to Mansfield Park to help out with the guys who were by then in the first XV. He came to a Tuesday evening training session, and I was overjoyed to see him there, part of the Hawick scene once again. But then the inevitable happened. The Scottish Rugby Union got to hear of this, and he was told in no uncertain terms to push off: as a professional, he had no right to be involved with an amateur club. I was furious and upset, for the man was an idol to me.

It is great to see the end of days like those, but whether we are better off now in terms of standards on the pitch seems doubtful. With promotion, relegation, personal advancement and cash rewards all inextricably linked to events on the field, it is inevitable that you will get some people behaving in a way that contravenes the entire ethos of the sport. Take the 2002 Heineken European Cup final, played in Cardiff. In the final minute of the match, Leicester were grimly defending near their own line, holding on to a precarious 15–9 lead. At a set scrum with the feed to Munster, who were within a converted try of winning the Cup, Leicester and England flanker Neil Back knocked the ball out of the hands of Munster scrum-half Peter Stringer. The referee was unsighted on the other side of the scrum, and the touch judge missed it. Leicester stole possession, cleared their lines and snatched victory.

Accuse me of being old-fashioned and out of touch if you like, but if you had done that when I was playing, you would have been read the riot act. Certainly you would have been ticked off by the committee and given a right good dressing-down. It is cheating, plain and simple. Various forms of cheating seem to have crept in since the advent of professionalism: front-row forwards pulling down a scrummage to kid the referee and get a penalty; players kicking ahead and then hurling themselves to the ground after even the softest contact with an opponent. It makes life very hard for referees.

People like Billy Burnet, who played against England at Inverleith in 1912 and was president of Hawick RFC – men of impeccable standards, upholders of the faith and of decency in rugby football – would have scorched us like a blow-torch if we had ever done anything of that kind. We had a deep respect bordering on fear for Billy, and we knew that there were certain things that he would not accept. Whether you were a good player, an ordinary player or the best in the world, if he didn't approve of something you did, he'd tell you. And believe me, you would know you'd been told. We'd never even have thought of doing what Back did. The fact that today players are not only thinking of it but actually going ahead and doing it is evidence of a decline in standards.

I was sad that Neil Back should be the culprit in that Cup final, because I had always had a tremendous respect for him. He carried the banner for flank forwards of smaller stature and made a tremendous impact on the game. But he let himself and his team down on that occasion.

One Scottish rugby tradition that anyone tries to change at his peril is the dedication of the whole of April to the sevens game. Beginning on the first Saturday of the month, there are tournaments each Saturday at Gala, Melrose, Hawick, Jedforest and Langholm, and always in that order. The Borders people love their day out at the sevens – they go down to the ground at about one o'clock in the afternoon, meet all their old friends and acquaintances, have a little lunch, a few beers, perhaps some tea or a wee dram, and watch the matches. In the old days there used to be a goal-kicking competition between the second semi-final and the final, and there were also flat races, handicap events involving local runners, which got tremendous support.

There are those in rugby who resent all this time being devoted to sevens just when the weather is starting to improve, and who feel the fifteen-a-side game should be allowed to benefit from spring sunshine after the gruelling winter months. But I don't think even an Act of the Scottish Parliament would persuade the locals to change their plans for those Saturdays. And it cannot be denied that the proceeds from the sevens events, which can be very handsome indeed, bring a much-needed boost to the coffers of the rugby clubs.

The flagship tournament, the Melrose Sevens, began in 1883, and although I am a Hawick man through and through, it has a special place in my heart because it was where I delivered my last-ever commentary in April 2002. I was happy that it all ended for me at a local event which I had always enjoyed watching. I remember my first visit there: my father and Uncle Joe took me in 1932, when I was eight years old, in Uncle Joe's Morris Cowley, one of those old cars with the bulbous noses. There were very few other cars around in our part of the world in those days, but that did not deter four or five thousand people from turning up at Melrose for the sevens by either bus or train or on foot. I think I must have first commentated on the tournament in 1954, six years before I switched to television and not that long after my first radio broadcast. No wonder I always found it unnerving.

Border people, and especially those in Melrose, pride themselves on having invented the game, and in fairness, at its best, it is a wonderful spectacle of fluent, flowing rugby, with space on the field in which players can exhibit their skills. Unfortunately, it also allows commentators to make complete oafs of themselves, unless they are very careful.

I don't know how many times I covered the Melrose Sevens but it was usually a nightmare, involving huge numbers of players I'd never seen before. Even when there were two Scottish teams playing, Jedforest and Edinburgh Academicals, say, you probably wouldn't know one of them. As I explained earlier, sevens is a tough test for any commentator because of the speed at which the games are played.

When I went to the Greenyards for my last-ever broadcast for BBC Scotland, I was given a reception similar to the one I had just experienced in Cardiff before my last-ever commentary on an international, so it was another very emotional day for me. I found it difficult to keep my composure when the whole crowd got to their feet and clapped. Someone said: 'Hey, it's you they're applauding,' and I had to stand up and acknowledge them. At least if you feel you have made the right decision it makes coping with the lump in the throat a little easier – and by the end of the day, I was absolutely convinced I'd done the correct thing in retiring, believe me! While everyone else was enjoying themselves, I was trying to survive the horrors of sevens commentary, attempting to identify players I had never clapped eyes on and keep up with everything going on at that hectic pace. No time for a shandy for the poor fool up in the commentary box, I'm afraid.

To play sevens is to subject yourself to a form of physical torture. It was always a fearsome test. Your throat became dry, and your legs felt weak after a while. You seemed to be in perpetual motion, hardly ever able to stop and draw breath. It may have been only seven minutes each way but it seemed more like half an hour, and half-time didn't appear to last for more than about ten seconds. If you ever want to punish somebody, get him to play sevens – it is the sport of sadists. But of course, if you come from my part of the world, it is supposed to be bred in the bones of every young lad. They're all expected to go rushing around each springtime like wee lambs in the field, tearing over the rugby field with only six team-mates for company, thinking only of winning the ball and inflicting on their opponents the kind of suffering they are enduring themselves when they don't have possession.

The ball is constantly moving and some surprising things can happen. Hugh McLeod, the tough Hawick prop forward, was good enough to move across one slot into the hooker's berth in a sevens scrum and play a full part in his team's performance. Hugh could handle the ball, run strongly, support his colleagues and tackle. You'd have thought all that was beyond the capability of a prop forward even in the fifteen-a-side game. It just goes to show how sevens allows players to hone different skills from those they are usually employing.

In the Borders, it has always been a matter of honour to beat the city slickers at sevens, so you can imagine the shock that went round the region when the London club Blackheath came up here, in 1958 I think it was, and won the Gala tournament. No one could believe it. But they had pace out wide and all their players seemed comfortable with the ball. That was what made them special; indeed, it is the hall-mark of all great sevens sides. They must have ball-players, footballers able to make decisions on the hoof and find subtle ways of unlocking a defence. That Blackheath team was also exceptional at covering the breadth of the pitch. We thought they were good, and they confirmed it when they went to Twickenham and won the prestigious Middlesex Sevens tournament a few weeks later.

I have always understood the attraction of the game to the Borders people. For so much of the winter season they see a series of dogfights, teams battling it out in mud, cold and rain. The opportunities for talented players to demonstrate their skills in that environment are few. The arrival of the sevens season marks the end of winter and the blooming of springtime. The trees are bursting into life, the colours are brightening on the hillsides and sevens, the game in which skills can be shown off, is played. It seems to go hand in hand with the changing of the season.

I loved playing for Hawick at all those Border clubs. I loved the nuggety forward battles, the attritional contests played out in thick mud and freezing cold rain. Somehow it was invigorating, stirring to the soul. At Hawick or Melrose, Gala or Jedforest, Kelso or Selkirk, and at countless others I have not mentioned, in all seasons and all weathers, as player or reporter or commentator, I have always received the warmest welcome and been treated to the kind of hospitality for which we like to think we are renowned in this part of Scotland. I've loved rugby all my life, and I will always be glad that it was my privilege to be involved with it in this wonderful Border region.

CHAPTER 10

THE DEATH OF JANIE

ALMOST ALL MY LIFE, I'VE KNOWN HAPPINESS AND personal success. My career was the fulfilment of my ambitions and more. Professionally, I achieved everything I had ever imagined from those earliest days when I used to sit on the wall in our street at home in Hawick, commentating on the efforts of my friends or on a big rugby international being played in my mind's eye.

Most importantly of all, I have a wonderful wife, whom I love now as much as when I first met her, and our lives were blessed further by the birth of our two beautiful daughters and, in time, lively, healthy grandchildren. Truly, our cup was running over.

But then Janie, our second daughter, died of cancer. In that moment, in April 2000, the sun set on a major part of us and our lives can never be the same again. I find it as painful to talk about today as on the day she passed away. They say that time heals all wounds, but that has not been our experience. Quite honestly, I do not expect it to be, either.

It is a truism that people who have never been through the same trauma and anguish cannot know what it is like to endure. They do their very best to comprehend it, so they can help friends or family in those circumstances. Bette and I are deeply grateful to the many people who wrote to us, expressing sadness and their best wishes, after Janie died, and I knew they meant well. But you feel that only those who have suffered a similar tragedy themselves can ever come close to understanding.

You cannot prepare yourself for it in any sense. The enormity of the loss dwarfs everything else in your life, and you hope and pray that somehow it can be avoided. But in far too many cases, the worst does happen and those who are left behind struggle to come to terms with their grief and sorrow.

Janie was a fantastic girl, a wonderful daughter. She was also a fine mother to two boys, James and Alex. We had seemed to have the perfect family. Both our daughters lived happy lives; both had married and had lovely, healthy children. We could have asked for nothing more. They were thoughtful towards us, sent us little gifts and always seemed to be there whenever we needed them or just wanted to have them around. I remember one present that arrived in the post from Janie when she was living in England. It was a record – 'I Just Called To Say I Love You' by Stevie Wonder. She explained that she wanted to send us something that would tell us, in song, that she was thinking of us; that even though she was living some distance away, her love for us remained strong. Bette and I were both so touched by that.

Sadly, that song now has something of a bitter-sweet resonance for us. I cannot bring myself to play it any more – it is too painful. I heard it suddenly start up on the radio the other day, without warning, and found myself sitting in our living room with tears cascading down my cheeks. When I went out into the kitchen, I discovered Bette in there, also howling, because she had heard it as well. We just couldn't help it, either of us.

Janie lifted everybody with whom she came into contact. All her friends tell us they loved her sense of fun, her gregariousness, her pretty, smiling face and her ability to make others laugh. These were in-fectious qualities, and people seemed to love just being around her, having her among them. Maybe it's a cliché but she was the life and soul of any party. She would pull your leg, too. It didn't matter whether she knew you or not, she would have a joke, have some fun with you.

I think another quality people admired in her was that she was a giving person. It was a wonderful talent. What gave her most pleasure was helping out, making others' lives that little bit easier, bringing a smile to their faces. If she was shopping with Bette and Bette admired something, the next thing she knew, Janie would have bought it for her.

Janie was the real livewire of the family, a proper comedienne, but that great sense of humour did not entirely mask her strong will and character. Because when Janie set her mind on something she invariably made sure that it happened. Inevitably, we had the odd disagreement here and there, but there was never any major bust-up. I had to do as I was told with three such strong women in the house. I had to watch myself for fear of being picked up on all manner of things. I remember Janie once coming round for Sunday lunch on the day after an international match. 'Dad,' she said, 'did you know that you used the word "pretty" nine times yesterday in your commentary? "Pretty good", "pretty strong", "pretty wild", "pretty high . . ."'

That brought me up short. I thought I'd made a

reasonably good job of it, and hadn't been aware of over-using the word. We all have our mannerisms, of course, but you have to be careful to avoid repeating stock phrases. I went away and reflected on that, and made sure I didn't make the same mistake again. That was Janie: she was always very straight, very forthright. She said it as she saw it, and you got a real blast sometimes. She was some lass, and a real, staunch Scot, too. 'Bring on the Springboks, bring on England,' she would say. She was super-confident and proud of her beloved Scotland.

Even when she became ill with the terrible disease that takes away so many of those we love, her qualities shone through, especially her courage, determination and love. She was still thinking about others, about how she could help ease the pain of her illness for them, what she could do to cheer them up and raise their morale. If you were looking for some-one to epitomise the bravery of all those people who do battle with this disease, then you would not need to look further than Janie. She never complained, never moaned, never said, 'Why me?' or anything like that. She just dealt with her treatment with the practicality and pragmatism that had always been part of her nature. She knew she was fighting for her life, and she was going to give it her best possible shot. Which is exactly what she did. Tragically, even that was not enough to save her.

Janie was sick for three years. Of course, during that time, there were a lot of awful lows, but there were some highs, too. At times, out of the darkness would come news that gave you reason to hope she might recover. At other times, the prognosis was grim. It was something we just had to live with day by day. You would open your eyes each morning and the first thing you thought about was your daughter. You would close your eyes at night to go to sleep, and the last thing on your mind was your daughter. And all through the days in between, try as you might, you couldn't stop wondering how she was, whether there was some better news, whether you might hear her cheery voice on the telephone telling you all was going to be well after all.

I was taught by my mother to go to church and pray, and I did that regularly as a young boy, but I have to concede that as I grew up and in later life my attendance lapsed somewhat. We're members of the Congregational Church here in Hawick, but I'm still a very poor attender. I am not someone who believes you can only be a Christian if you go to church every week, or that, if you do attend regularly, it necessarily makes you a good Christian or a good representative of whatever religion you follow. I think it is in our everyday lives that we demonstrate whether or not we are a Christian person. You can devote yourself to helping others and yet never go near a church in your whole life. Would that not make you a good Christian in God's eyes? I suspect it would.

Janie always put others before herself, and in my understanding of religion, her values were Christian values. When she became ill, I have to admit I was very resentful and I had to struggle hard to hold on to what Christianity I did have within my soul. I felt that if there was a God, surely He would see to it that someone so good, who had so much to give and who had lived such a selfless life, would be spared. I managed to cling on by acknowledging that we hadn't been singled out in some way. As Bette says, you tend to think you are the only people who go through this awful suffering, yet almost every family in the country has to endure it at some time or other. Still I found it hard to accept Janie's illness, and the fact that she should be confronting death at such a young age.

Both Bette and I know now that she kept it from us for as long as she possibly could. That was her way. She wouldn't have wanted to cause us any anxiety if she didn't have to, and like the rest of us, she hoped, of course, she would get better. When I first heard the news, I simply couldn't believe it. We'd seen her just a few days earlier and she had looked no different. Maybe a little tired and a shade drawn, but with a busy life and two young boys to bring up, that was only to be expected from time to time.

Janie had met the TV racing commentator Derek Thompson while working in London as a studio manager with the BBC. They married and moved to north Yorkshire, where the boys were born. James was ill for the early part of his life with kidney trouble and eventually one kidney had to be removed to allow the other to strengthen. But he now lives a full and active life.

After a time, Janie and Derek moved again, to Chalfont St Giles in Buckinghamshire, where she became a successful aerobics instructor. But sadly, their marriage ran into trouble and, although Janie tried hard to save it, they broke up a few years later. The stress of the divorce took its toll. Eventually, she moved back to Edinburgh with the boys, qualified in massage and aromatherapy and took classes in aquarobics and went on to join Lothian & Edinburgh Enterprise, becoming involved in their Investors in People programme. She was popular, worked hard and made a lot of good friends. The boys went to Stewart's Melville College in the city and she wanted to live close by, so she bought a flat right opposite the college. Determined and practical as ever, evidently she was already planning for the possibility that her sons might have to face the future without her by ensuring that they would have a convenient base when they were older.

We looked forward to her visits to Hawick. She would come in, smiling, laughing and chattering away brightly. But then one day she sat us down and told us what was going on. I felt as if I was listening to some conversation from another world, another family's problem. I couldn't believe we were talking about Janie. Her bravery in confronting the disease came as no surprise to Bette and me, because she had always been a fighter, a fiery wee battler against anything that obstructed her path. But we were absolutely devastated. We retired to a quiet corner of our home and sat there with heavy hearts. Despite Janie's optimism, we knew that she had a real fight on her hands this time.

As a parent, it is your worst nightmare. I found it impossible to sift the dreadful mixture of dismay, anger, bewilderment, fear and love that I felt into any sort of order in my mind. I didn't know much about cancer, but the very word creates fear in the minds of most people and we were no different in that respect. I had little idea of what lay ahead of her and whether she would survive it. I've always been a bit of a worrier anyway, and the sheer sense of helplessness was just overwhelming. Along with the anguish, there is a great desire within you to do something of real value to help improve the situation, but there is simply nothing you can do. Time, dragging by slowly and painfully, has to be allowed to take its course, punctuated by the drugs and therapy used to try to kill the disease. That is just so hard.

Even harder was watching Janie grow progressively weaker. Here was a fit, active, healthy mother of two, who had always possessed boundless energy and enthusiasm, gradually losing a little bit more strength day by day. It was awful to see. We hoped against hope that the treatment would work and we grieved for her while she was undergoing it. Undoubtedly radiotherapy and chemotherapy do save lives, but they are extremely tough tests of endurance in themselves and take a heavy toll.

At least we knew Janie was in good hands. She had a marvellous consultant at the Western General Hospital in Edinburgh, Professor Smyth. She was very fond of him and he took great care of her. She was also full of praise for the kind nursing staff on Ward 1, and others who administered chemotherapy. The staff at Maggie's Centre, where Janie gained great comfort, were also very supportive.

I think we began to realise just how serious her illness was when we went up to Edinburgh one day to see her. I left Bette with Janie while I went to cover a match for the BBC and the *Glasgow Herald*. They were planning to go for a walk that afternoon. But when I got back in the evening, I discovered that there had been no walk. Janie had wanted to go, but when it came to it, she just did not have the strength. The mind was willing, as ever, but the body was failing. She had already become very slow in her walking but now she found she could not walk at all.

All this, of course, affected Linda greatly. They were very close. As girls, they had always talked about what they would do when they were older and the families they both wanted to have when they grew up. They were going to do all sorts of things together. We found out later that Janie had told Linda much more about her illness, and much earlier, than she had told us. It wasn't that she wanted to keep things from us, just that, as she said to Linda, she didn't want Mum and Dad worrying about her. We were really blessed to have two such wonderful daughters who were such devoted sisters, too.

It was really tough for me trying to work each Saturday afternoon, not to mention going off on a Thursday evening when the Six Nations Championship came round. Quite honestly, the main reason I kept going was because Janie herself insisted on it. I remember going up to Edinburgh to stay with her one weekend, and on the Saturday morning, I said I thought I would pull out of the match that afternoon. Janie, in her usual feisty mode, was having none of it. 'You have to go,' she said. 'It's your job. You have a commitment. Don't even think about not going.' That put me in my place. I trotted meekly off to the match without another word. Janie was always determined to keep her promises and honour her commitments, and she expected her family to do likewise.

When I was commentating, I couldn't allow my work to be affected, because that wouldn't have done anyone any good. So I just tried to concentrate on the job in hand for the hour and a half or so I was on air. They say that we are born with a complex, intricate mind which can store untold amounts of stuff and yet focus on just one thing at a time even when there may be all kinds of other problems demanding its attention. I guess the brain must be like an enormous filing cabinet from which you can select certain pieces of information or files on a particular subject at a given moment. Whatever the explanation, I managed it somehow. Inevitably, though, Janie's situation was always there at the back of my mind. How could it have been otherwise?

It is said that it is perhaps only in adversity that you find out who your true friends are. That was certainly the case with us. To start with, Janie's positive attitude, her belief that the treatment would work and all would be well, boosted us enormously. But in addition to that, the support we received from so many friends was almost overwhelming. I would like them to know that their love, their good wishes and their kindness were a great source of comfort to us in the dark times. It cannot take away the pain you are feeling, but the knowledge that there were so many people with us, praying for Janie and willing her to get better, was an inspiring thing for Bette and me. It meant Janie was not fighting that illness alone. Her friends from the boys' school were absolutely wonderful to the whole family; all her friends, even people who had not known her very long, rallied round and helped us to keep going.

After two years, two long years tinged variously by

hope and despair, darkness and bright interludes, Janie learned that the cancer had spread. She did not tell us, not then. I would say it was only in her last few months that we really knew how bad things were. As she became steadily weaker, so it became apparent to us that things were not working out, that the treatment probably wasn't achieving what we had been hoping and praying for. While she was still there, fighting mentally, there was always hope. She was not going to give up and we certainly weren't. She wouldn't have let us, anyway. She'd have been angry, and given us some fierce words, if we had shown signs of throwing in the towel. She remained strong in her mind right to the end.

Even just a few months before she died, and right in the middle of her debilitating treatment, Janie attended a social evening, a dress-up dinner, and she looked lovely. We have a photograph of her, with Scott, the very nice young man she had met some time after she and Derek had broken up, and they made a handsome couple. If you had met her that night, you would never have imagined she had so little time left.

But the evidence of her physical decline could not be denied. I lost count of the number of times I lay in bed at night, my mind twisting and turning, agonising about how all this had come out of nothing to hit my family, what it all meant and how it was all going to end. You can help to resolve most bad situations yourself through your own will and determination. You can work hard to solve financial difficulties, you can call on your inner strength to get over other kinds of misfortune. But in these circumstances you are absolutely powerless.

I looked at this beautiful figure lying in her hospital bed, with her great big brown eyes that had always been so full of vitality, and just felt overwhelmed by the enormity of what was happening. Janie's friends began to arrive from all over the country, some from even further afield, to see her, talk to her, just to be with her. I know that having them there, hearing them express their love, meant a lot to her. Derek, her former husband, came up from England, and Scott was constantly by her side. Seeing Scott there, and knowing they might have married had things been different, was almost unbearably poignant for Bette and me.

Janie was in hospital for about a month before the end, knowing that she would never come out again. A month is a long time in those circumstances. But still, drained as she was of almost all her energy, she was busy making arrangements for the boys, talking to them, trying to help them cope. It was as though she could not let go until she had completed this task. It was perhaps her final duty on this earth and one of her most important. And as with everything else she did, she gave it everything she had.

The day she died was a Saturday, the day of the Scottish Cup final at Murrayfield. I feared the end was near and I was not going to go, but even on what was to turn out to be the last day of her life, Janie was adamant. There was no way she'd let me off the hook. So I took my orders, went to work and commentated on the game, but I did so with a terribly heavy heart. For probably the only time in my life, I confess I did not have my soul in the commentary. I did it, I got through it, but that was all. As soon as the match was over I raced back to the hospital.

I was too late. Janie had finally closed her eyes at around two o'clock that afternoon, with Bette, Linda and Alan at her side. I had been sitting in a commentary box while my daughter had died. I regret having left the hospital now, obviously. I know it could have happened at any time, and that her mother, sister and brother-in-law had been with her, but I cannot begin to describe how awful I felt that I wasn't there too. My only crumb of consolation, if that it can be called, is that it was what Janie had wanted.

The tumours had been spreading to different parts of Janie's body. The doctors told us that the worst one was close to her heart, and it was this that killed her. You may know it is coming, you might have had a long time to prepare yourself, to steel yourself, if you like, for that day, but none of it means anything whatsoever when it finally comes. Nothing can prepare you for it. Bette and I cried and cried. Our hearts were broken.

People came from far and wide for Janie's funeral service, testimony to what they thought of her – a variety of lovely people she had drawn together as her friends during her life. We asked them all to wear a colour, not black. We wanted to celebrate her life, not her death. But we were shattered, naturally, and I don't know how we got through that day. We appreciate how very lucky we are to have Linda and Alan and all the grandchildren, and we love them all dearly, but I have to say I don't think we will ever get over Janie's death. I know you shouldn't be, but I have to admit that I am still very resentful about losing her. So much good in her was lost while so much evil carries on in the world. It is not something you can really ever come to terms with.

Perhaps the younger generation provided a chink of light at the end of a very long, dark tunnel. Janie's son, Alex, who was only eighteen, stood up at the funeral service and spoke from the heart about his mum, and it was beautiful. I so admired that boy and his enormous courage that day. It is something I will never forget as long as I live. His words touched everyone, so much so that at the end of his tribute, everybody quite spontaneously applauded. It was the first time, many people told us, they had ever seen everybody at a funeral service do that. It was a tragic occasion, all right, but at the same time a wonderful, somehow uplifting experience.

Courage and bravery, it was clear, had not died with Janie. She had handed on those qualities to her sons. James, who was only fifteen, also showed extraordinary depths of courage in the way he handled the loss of his mum. Linda looked after the boys after Janie died. Alex had finished school but continued his studies in Edinburgh. James moved to Alan and Linda's home in Dollar, a forty-minute drive from Edinburgh, and attended the Academy there, renowned as a seat of learning but also possessed of a beautiful, small, caring community spirit which I am sure helped him a lot. James has finished school now and shares the flat his mum bought for them with

Alex – just as Janie planned, although we didn't know that until it was all over. They are fine, good-living, upstanding young men, and we're hugely proud of them.

We continue to grieve for Janie, but I know what she would say if she read this. 'Oh, don't be silly, Dad. Carry on, make the best of life, enjoy the years of your retirement. Never mind what happened.' I'm afraid Bette and I find it impossible to adopt that approach. It's no good telling us that it is the best policy, the only way forward. When you get older, you find it hard sometimes to follow what conventional thinking may dictate or suggest. We have had two beautiful daughters in our lives whom we love to bits, and one of them was taken away from us in the prime of her life. We cannot move on from that huge loss.

We try to be cheerful, to show happiness on the outside. But deep down, the pain will not go away. Not a single day goes by when we don't think about Janie, and I don't believe there'll ever be one. We miss her and we always will.

CHAPTER 11
LIFE NOW

I WILL BE EIGHTY-ONE IN OCTOBER 2004, AND I sometimes wonder what on earth happened to all those years. You don't feel that old. In your mind you are always the same age. However, there is no denying the limitations the march of time imposes on your body. It irks me that I've lost about twenty yards off my drive at golf, which means I am now seriously beginning to doubt my capacity to topple that fellow Tiger Woods from the summit of the world game. Those ambitions aside, it just makes golf such a struggle if you're not driving the full distance.

When the British Open is held on one of the beautiful Scottish courses, we usually go up for a day or two to watch Tiger and his colleagues steer the ball around them. I love St Andrews, naturally – the home of golf and surely one of the most charismatic courses anywhere in the world. With its testing runs and hollows, its devilish bunkers and the wind that is more often than not tearing at your sleeves like some child demanding attention, it is the ultimate challenge. I've seen some of the world's greatest players almost reduced to the level of local club hackers by conditions that can quickly become torturous up on the east coast of Scotland.

The wind blows just as hard at Royal Troon, on the other side of the country, except that over there it comes straight off the Atlantic Ocean. Some of those fellows from countries like Australia and Fiji find themselves trying to play their rounds bundled up in so many sweaters that they have to adapt to a different kind of game.

Each of the major Scottish courses, whether you are talking about St Andrews, Royal Troon, Carnoustie, Muirfield, Gleneagles, Loch Lomond or wherever, offers its own unique resistance to the golfer. And links golf, of course, is always a separate test in itself as you try to keep the ball low into the wind and negotiate it round the natural obstacles in your path.

For me, golf is a wonderful game, a great test of a human being's skill, patience, resolve under pressure and ability to accept the days when simply everything goes wrong. If you can retain a sense of equilibrium after all that, then you must have a pretty cool head on your shoulders. Handling the pressure, both physical and mental, is an integral part of the attraction of golf. You need to stay calm and not lose your rag or your self-control.

I've played the game all my life. I was brought up in the faith, for my dad was a keen golfer. I first picked up a club on a family holiday as a wee lad, and my father and I had a round of golf every day on our holidays after that. At home, as a schoolboy, as soon as four o'clock came on spring and summer evenings I was away on my bicycle up the hill and on to the first tee of our local course.

Dad taught me to enjoy the game and to do my best but to adhere to its customs: courtesy to your opponent, good manners on the course, fair play and decency in your own behaviour. I am pleased and encouraged to see that generally speaking, these standards continue to underpin golf, which I'm sure must be a factor in its popularity. Newcomers to the sport accept the rules and continue its traditions, and I applaud those in charge for their refusal to countenance any lowering of those high standards over the years. If only we could say the same of all sports, not to mention other areas of society in general.

Ours is a hillside golf course and I find it harder and harder to clamber up those hills. They leave me a bit short of breath so I find myself having to wait for what seems like ages before I can actually play my shot. That is frustrating when you can vividly remember a time when you would hardly have noticed the slope, let alone been puffing along like some old steam train. But there it is. It's a similar story if you get off the fairway and end up in some of that tufty stuff or heather that some courses like to put in your way. How anyone can derive any pleasure from seeing some poor innocent out for a nice day on the course with friends get waylaid like a wee fly in the spider's web, I don't know. By the time you have hacked your way out of that, the relaxed mood has certainly evaporated.

I find it enough of a challenge these days to hit that little white ball. When you miss a shot or play it poorly, or the luck goes against you with the bounce or run of the ball, it's an excuse for what we call 'having a girn', a right old moan. I'm always complaining that I am not playing well enough. Mind you, Bette reckons that even if I went round the Hawick course in 59, I'd still complain about something, such as missing an easy putt, or driving waywardly at the ninth. She's probably right, too.

The best round I ever put together on the Hawick course was a 69. I holed everything that day. I have had two holes-in-one: the first at the short par-4 sixteenth and another at the 170-yard par-3 eighteenth with a 4-iron. Both planned, of course. But, sad to say – and just to put that fellow Woods's mind at rest – those were red-letter days.

I was never a startling putter, but pretty steady. At one time, I was playing some pretty good golf and would have been disappointed if I'd gone round in more than 73 or 74, and my handicap has been as low as 6. It's 12 now. The trouble is, I am inconsistent. I just don't put together enough good holes. I once started off a round up at Hawick with the following scores on my card: 3, 18, 4, 4, 3. The green at the second runs flush with the road and I put four balls on the other side of it, so I was playing 9 before I'd even left the tee! The worst thing about it was that the incident found its way into the local paper and as a result I had my leg pulled mercilessly for months afterwards. I consoled myself with the thought that I had done something on a golf course that not even Colin Montgomerie had achieved.

The Selkirk club, not far from my home, has a delightful course with some marvellous views and scenery, so if you're in for a bit of sightseeing, then it's the spot to be. If you're hoping to play a round of golf without suffering too much torment, then I'd say be wary. It can trap the unsuspecting and make complete fools of them. There is heather all over it, and it can be a beast, especially when the wind is blowing. We don't go for heather in the Borders as a rule, but Selkirk has got the full works. When I've played it I've been fortunate to get out alive. There are all sorts of strange holes – well, strange to me anyway – with greens about as big as postage stamps located in awkward positions. Just trying to stop your ball on them is difficult enough, never mind trying to sink your putt.

Of all the courses I have played in my lifetime, my favourite would have to be Gullane, near Muirfield. It is one of the courses they use for qualifying for the Open Championship, so its quality and many fascinating challenges can be taken as read. Another point in its favour is its scenery. Playing there, with the sea right beside the course, and the Forth and the hills leading up to Edinburgh in the background, is pure joy. Bette and I were playing the number one course at Gullane once and I hit off at the seventh tee. I started walking after my ball, got halfway down the fairway and suddenly realised Bette was not there. When I looked back up the fairway to the tee, she was still standing there, looking in completely the other direction, entranced by the view. Well, as she said, it was better than watching my attempts to keep my drive on the straight and narrow.

Most of our family play golf. Bette was no mean player in her time and once won a ladies' competition, while Linda had a hole-in-one at Tobermory in June 2003. The grandchildren all play too, even Linda's young daughter, Lindsay. I still have a game every Thursday, weather permitting, with Harry Whitaker, a good friend of mine who played scrumhalf for Hawick and the South of Scotland. Harry went on to rugby league, but returned when his career was over to Hawick, where he is now a physiotherapist. I have only ever beaten him twice, he's so annoyingly good, and I joke with him that his battered body will one day be found on the thirteenth hole at our club.

The great thing about golf is that it is something you can carry on enjoying as you get older, even if you are not as good at it as you were in your youth. I don't get nearly as uptight and angry if I play a poor shot nowadays as I did when I was younger. At my time of life you have to try to be philosophical. Indeed, perhaps the word that best sums up old age is frustration. Your inability to do as many things as you used to do – and to do those you can still do as quickly and satisfactorily as was once the case – can be so infuriating.

My home in Hawick is on the top of a hill overlooking part of the town. The trees are wonderful, the colours too, especially in autumn. What can be less than wonderful is the steep climb up to it. Bette still goes up and down it regularly on foot and claims it keeps her in robust health. I just take her word for it and use the car. I am not afraid of growing old, but I would not like to be incapacitated to the extent that I couldn't move from A to B on my own. I think most people feel that way. Once you lose your mobility, it can become a struggle to keep your spirits up. I admire people who manage to keep cheerful in those circumstances. If it happened to me I would just have to adjust, but it's not an appealing prospect.

Usually the first faculty to decline is your memory. That can have unexpectedly pleasing results – you may be able to convince yourself that Scotland always beat England in those titanic struggles of yesteryear – but for the most part it is another frustration. The majority of my contemporaries bemoan the fact that their memory is no longer as sharp as it was. You begin to wonder whether you have said something to somebody before and they are perhaps too polite to point this out. You can only hope not. You can also only hope that this development is simply a natural part of the ageing process, rather than the advent of some awful degenerative illness such as Alzheimer's disease, which is the great fear of all of us of advancing years. You would not wish the cruelties and indignities that brings on your worst enemy.

I have certainly noticed this loss of sharpness in myself. As I explained earlier, my feeling that my memory and my reactions were not quite as quick as they once were was a critical factor in my decision to finish my broadcasting career. I didn't want people sitting at home listening to me and remarking to each other, 'Hey – he just said that five minutes ago.' No thank you very much. Nobody ever told me that this had happened, but I didn't want to hang around until it did.

When I did retire, I was hardly at a loose end. I seemed to be inundated with all kinds of testimonial dinners, awards and calls asking me to do this or that. After a fair few months of it, I told Bette one day that perhaps I shouldn't have retired after all – it was too much like hard work. I felt so honoured, but it was all a bit overwhelming. The kindness of people throughout the rugby-playing world was extraordinary. I had letters, poems, musical compositions, messages of support – all sorts of things – from folk in all the leading rugby nations, but especially Scotland; letters from complete strangers, saying how sad they were that I would no longer be commentating, thanking me for what I had done for the game and telling me how much they had enjoyed my coverage. Those letters touched my heart. I really hadn't expected anything like that. It was nice to know that I had added to people's enjoyment of watching rugby matches. I think all my fellow professional commentators who at one time worked on BBC Sport, people like Harry Carpenter, Peter O'Sullevan, Peter Bromley, David Coleman, Ron Pickering and Kenneth Wolstenholme, would agree with my sentiments. To have people say of you after your retirement that you helped their enjoyment of sport on television is all that you could ever have hoped for.

As the poor postman struggled manfully to our door, day after day, to unload his sack, like Santa Claus on Christmas Eve, I imagined what my dear father would have said. I doubt whether he'd have believed it, nor could I. I am so grateful to all those wonderful people who took such trouble to send me presents, cards or thanks for the past and good wishes for the future. Whenever a long involvement like that comes to an end there are inevitably pangs of sadness, and all those thoughtful gestures from so many different people not only eased that sense of loss but gave me a wealth of mementos of my career. They meant the world to me.

People everywhere were so kind that at times I found it almost too much for me. The Variety Club of Great Britain gave me a special award and I was very chuffed with that. To receive such an accolade from a body representing the entire broadcasting industry is the ultimate in my eyes. Then there was a special night for the International Rugby Hall of Fame at the Lancaster Hotel in central London. I had been inducted into the Hall of Fame in October 2001, and it is one of the biggest honours that ever came my way through my broadcasting work, for I was the first member to be elected without having been capped for my country. They organised this celebration dinner after I retired and *The Times* newspaper, which had asked me to pick my best World XV, invited along all the players I had chosen. It was a wonderful occasion. Players I had not seen for decades turned up, almost every one of my team – I think the former South African forward Frik du Preez and David Campese were the only ones unable to be there.

I picked Du Preez and Colin Meads of New Zealand as my locks on the basis that nobody would dare manhandle them, which people seemed to think was fair enough; another of my choices, however, stirred up a real hornet's nest of debate. Rob Andrew of England might not have been the greatest running fly-half the world had ever seen, but I reckoned that as a strategist, a player who could run a whole game superbly and effectively, he would take an awful lot of beating. He was good enough for me, so in he went. The trouble was, during his career Andrew had put Scotland to the sword many times, which made him *persona non grata* north of the border, so I had calls almost day and night about that selection. Irate former army colonels from the Highlands and gruff ex-labourers from heaven knows where were on the phone or sending me letters. 'Have ye gone mad in your old age?' was the general drift. But I am quite happy to stick by my decision.

Less controversially (in the sense that, as it deals with an experience that is unique to yours truly, there can be no arguments!), I am often asked which of all the matches I covered was the most memorable for me as a commentator. From a purely personal point of view, it would have to be the 1976 Five Nations Championship game at Murrayfield in which

Scotland beat England 22–12 – and in which Alan Lawson, the Scotland scrum-half, scored two tries. There can't be anything much more exciting for a commentator than to witness his own son-in-law flying for the line from forty yards out. People told me many times during my career that they appreciated the fact that I didn't get over-excited when I was broadcasting, but that day, I'm afraid, must have been an exception.

And what about that tremendous 1973 match between Barbarians and New Zealand at Cardiff, which turned out to be arguably the greatest ever in terms of a sustained series of sweeping, attacking moves? Well, that was the most memorable match I *didn't* commentate on, to my everlasting regret. At times, the Barbarians' play was simply breathtaking. The early try, started beneath the shadow of his posts by Phil Bennett and finished so thrillingly with a dive into the corner at the other end of the pitch by Gareth Edwards, set the tone for a wonderful advertisement for the game at its best.

Not only was I not commentating – I wasn't even at the Arms Park to see that historic performance. Cliff Morgan was the commentator that day. He had covered the 1971 Lions tour to New Zealand, from which most of that All Blacks side had been drawn, and so was ideally equipped to provide coverage of the Cardiff game. Cliff did a super job, too. But I have to admit that when I saw the game on television I fervently wished I had been involved. It was a real sizzler!

It is a shame that we don't see nowadays more of the Barbarians' ethos: to entertain as well as to win. In fact you always had the feeling with the Barbarians that the entertainment took priority over all else. We owe a debt of gratitude to that wandering side for reminding us of what is possible in the way of thrilling, handling rugby played by men prepared to tilt their lances in daring attack. Sadly, Barbarians-style rugby is much harder to achieve in the modern game, because, as I have discussed, creating an incision in defence is so difficult. Sometimes you long for a flash of that old spirit; for players to say 'Let's have a go' rather than 'Don't try that, it's too dangerous.'

I talked earlier about my fondness for Cardiff and about how pleased I was to have delivered my last international commentary there. Given my admiration for the rugby and people of Wales, I was particularly touched when, on my retirement, I was presented with an award from the Welsh Rugby Union. The inscription read: 'Presented to Bill

McLaren by the Wales team on the occasion of his retirement from broadcasting in recognition of his wonderful contribution to rugby football.' As if that wasn't enough, I then received another gift from Wales, from the *Western Mail*, the Welsh morning newspaper based in Cardiff, bearing the message: 'Thanks for a memorable career from all your friends in Wales.' Wasn't that lovely?

From my own countrymen, I had already been thrilled to accept a beautiful crystal rugby ball, in recognition of my long service to rugby football, which was presented to me before one of my last commentaries at Murrayfield by Her Royal Highness the Princess Royal. It was a hell of a cold day, with one of those icy winds blowing around the stadium which seemed to have come straight off the snow-capped Pentland Hills. The Princess had been out on the field a wee while, meeting various dignitaries, and she must have been half-frozen. When it was my turn to go out, I thought to myself, if I walk all this way, she'll be shaking with cold by the time I reach her. So I ran. Of course, I then arrived in front of her all puffed out and had to catch my breath before I could speak!

I got on awfully well with the Princess. I admire her tremendously, and have always found her a lovely, cheery person with no airs or graces about her at all. She does a lot of good work for charity, much of it unseen and unacknowledged. Her rugby-playing son Peter had been a member of a Scottish Schools side that toured South Africa, along with my grandson Gregor Lawson.

Once I'd got my breath back, I asked the Princess: 'Have you seen your son yet this morning?' She said that she hadn't.

'Well, Ma'am, he was out with our grandson last night, and God help him if he was in his company.'

She laughed her head off. I thought she was super.

All these marvellous tributes . . . and still there was one more to come. I was staggered when I was informed in 2003 that I was to be invested with the CBE by Her Majesty the Queen. No wonder I was starting to feel overwhelmed by the level of attention. The medal, awarded for what was termed services to sports broadcasting, completed a distinguished hat-trick for me. Back in the 1980s I had been given the MBE and then, in the mid 1990s, the OBE.

The CBE was to be presented to me by the Queen herself at the Palace of Holyroodhouse in Edinburgh. Of the twenty-two investitures held each year, most take place at Buckingham Palace, where I received my MBE and OBE – there are only one or two in

Edinburgh (and occasionally one at Cardiff Castle in Wales), so I was pleased to be among the select band of eighty recipients honoured in Scotland on 3 July.

We had been to one previous royal event at Holyroodhouse: a Queen's garden party. Janie had accompanied Bette and me on that occasion and had completely stolen the show. Protocol dictates that you do not speak to the Queen unless and until she speaks to you first, but Janie had little time for that sort of stuffy rigmarole. Without waiting for the Queen to address her, she said to her: 'I see your horse won at Royal Ascot, Ma'am.'

The royal staff were all looking round to see who it was who had dared breach protocol, but one person who wasn't in the least bothered was the Queen. She responded graciously straight away. Janie knew a lot about horses through her then husband, Derek Thompson, and she and the Queen chatted away perfectly naturally about them for a few minutes. I was quite miffed. After all, I was supposed to be the one there to be presented to the Queen, but once Janie had engaged her in conversation, Her Majesty completely ignored me. Daughters!

I was pretty nervous when I went up to meet Her Majesty at the Palace of Holyroodhouse. Probably nearly everyone is: you are anxious that you might put your foot in it somehow, do the wrong thing, or say something embarrassing. I don't feel very at ease done up in top hat and tails at the best of times – I am not a great one for dressing up – and there is a very definite formal atmosphere inside the Picture Gallery, where the investitures take place. You can feel the sense of occasion – and the nervous tension. So although it was a very special experience, I must say I was mightily relieved to get it over without mishap. I was quite glad to get home, take off the morning suit and climb into my old, comfortable gardening gear.

Finally, all the excitement levelled off and I was able to settle down to my retirement. I still get a lot of calls inviting me to speak at dinners, but to tell you the truth, it is not something I have ever fancied doing. In fact I quake at the thought of it. People assume that if you have made a career of broadcasting live to millions you will be a natural for the after-dinner circuit. But talking into a microphone is completely different: for a start, nobody in your audience is looking at you. I have to do the occasional turn, but I try to keep them to a minimum. For example, I did deliver a speech to raise money for a hospital treatment room when Janie was ill. But I had to force myself even to do that, and I certainly didn't enjoy it. I must have turned down thousands of pounds in declining these invitations, but I don't regret that. I have no desire to subject myself to the kind of stress it involves. It is not as if I'm desperate to go to rugby dinners at all, even as a non-participating guest: as I've said, I'm not a great socialiser. I don't want to offend anybody, but the truth is I'm happier at home with my wife.

I have done a lot of travelling around in my life, in the UK and abroad, but Scotland is where I have always wanted to spend most of my time, and as I get older, that is increasingly the case. Scotland has always had its own identity – Scots generally have a reputation for saying what they think, and there is nothing wrong with that – and I'm delighted to have seen that individualism recognised with the emergence of our own Parliament in recent years. In my view it is a good thing that we have our own people looking after our affairs. When policy was dictated from London, you could hardly say it was decided by those who knew Scotland best. Well-meaning they may have been, but surely it is better that our own politicians formulate our policy. I believe our political leaders have sufficient maturity to chart the right path ahead for us. Links to neighbouring countries, especially England, will always be strong, and it is right that they should be. All the same, I welcome the chance we have to take our own nation into the twenty-first century. Scotland is a great place and we have some exceptional young people growing up in it. And for a wee country, with naturally limited resources, I'd say we punch well above our weight, in sport as in other areas of life.

Most of the other parts of the world I have visited regularly have been rugby-playing countries, for obvious reasons. Since rugby is a minority sport in the USA, that great nation was never on my working itinerary, and until relatively recently I had never set foot on American soil. So Bette and I decided to rectify that omission a few years ago by taking a short holiday in New York – and we did so in some style, flying out on Concorde and sailing home on the *QE2*. Both legs of the journey were the experiences of a lifetime, especially flying through the skies in that beautiful plane. The power at take-off made even those fearsome French forward packs of the 1970s look powder-puffy by comparison. The surge of the engines and the G-forces it generated nearly buried you in your leather seat. It felt as if you might almost be driven through the back of it and into the knees of the fellow sitting behind you, so strong was the forward propulsion. The air was so clear that when we climbed up to 60,000 feet, which was the cruising altitude for Concorde, the plane barely wobbled. Another surge of power was clearly discernible when the aircraft hit mach 2 speed, twice the speed of sound. We landed in New York after only three and a half hours of supersonic luxury. It was without question one of the great moments of our lives. It was such a shame when that amazing aeroplane, painstakingly created by British and French workers, was finally taken out of service in October 2003. The costs made it no longer practical, they said, but it is always sad to see the demise of any magnificent invention.

I had a particular reason for choosing New York. As a child, I had been very keen on boxing, as I was on all sports, and one of my heroes was the great American world champion Joe Louis. They called him the Brown Bomber, and the description was about right because he had two fists that exploded like bombs into the bodies and faces of his opponents. Talk about being hit by a truck. In fact, that would probably have been preferable to walking into a Joe Louis right-hander.

On 22 June 1938, when I was fourteen, Louis met the German boxer Max Schmeling, the darling of the German leader, Adolf Hitler, at New York's Yankee

Stadium. They were by some distance the two best fighters of their time. In front of 70,000 people, Louis knocked out his rival after just two minutes and four seconds of the first round to take the world title and gain revenge for Schmeling's victory over him exactly two years earlier. A single right from the Brown Bomber smashed so hard into the German's body that it broke two bones, forcing his third lumbar vertebra into his kidney. Schmeling is said to have screamed so loudly that it sounded as if his cry was coming from the back of the hall. Far away in Scotland, at some ungodly hour, a lad had crept downstairs in his dressing gown to join his father in the sitting room. Together we huddled closer to the wireless. The static came and went, like the waves under a ship, but I could make out the key moments in what was to become known as one of the great fights of all time.

So one of the first things I did when we arrived in New York was to take a cab to the world-famous scene of that big fight, and of so many others down the years. I stood there transfixed by the enormous stadium that was so familiar to me but which I had never seen in the flesh, as it were. There wasn't any-one around, so I was able to drink it all in quietly on my own – all the history, the dramas, the great nights, the crowds and the noise. It was a moment I shall never forget as long as I live.

My favourite southern-hemisphere country of those I visited on my travels is probably South Africa – it is a country of such rich variety. When I went there in 1994, Bette and Janie came with me, and once the rugby was over we all flew from Johannesburg to Malamala to spend a few days in a beautiful old house.

One evening we went into the bush on what they call a 'sundowner' trip, timed to give you the opportunity to see one of those magnificent African sunsets. We stopped out in the middle of nowhere as the sun slipped slowly below the horizon, turning the sky into a riot of colour. A bottle or two of wine, which our guides had packed into the jeep, were opened and we just sat there watching this beautiful event. But not even that marvellous sunset was as impressive a sight as what followed. As the sky grew dark, we were driving slowly back through the bush when one of our guides, Peter, suddenly asked the driver to stop and urged the rest of us to remain still and quiet. We did so, allowing the magical sounds of the animals and birds of Africa to wash over us for a moment. Then we saw what it was that had prompted Peter's instructions. Straight in front of our jeep was a pride of lions. We sat there, rigid, hardly daring to breathe, and gazed at these big, yellow eyes staring right back at us from out of the darkness. Deciding that we were not a threat, the lions came closer and we were able to make out the shapes of a male proudly leading his lionesses and a couple of cubs across the bush just yards in front of us. We were absolutely enchanted. In the rapt silence, all that could be heard was the sound of my knees knocking.

In several more days on safari we saw what they describe as the 'big five' African animals: lions, elephants, Cape buffalo, rhinos and leopards. It was an enthralling experience, and one I will always savour.

We were back in South Africa a couple of years later, when our grandson Gregor toured the country with the Scottish Schools squad, and this time the entire family came along. Janie and Linda took the four youngest children to Botswana for a safari holiday, and then joined up with Bette at Sun City for two days, while Alan and I were working. We all met up in Cape Town to watch the rugby and then followed the Garden Route for a few days before heading on to Durban. It is a memory I treasure: being able to share the unique experience of that amazing country with my whole, beloved family.

When I think about it, perhaps the words 'unique experience' sum up my whole life. Because it certainly has been a unique experience. I have known happiness and sadness, achievement and failure. I have endured three terrible events that have brought tremendous heartache: the death of Janie, our daughter, a war and a major illness. But they have been balanced by three wonderful blessings that have been at the core of my life. The first is the times I have shared with Bette, my adorable wife. I could never have found a better, lovelier or kinder person with whom to spend my days. The second is the joy brought to us first by our two beautiful daughters and then by our five marvellous grandchildren. And the third is the great times I have known as a rugby commentator, living out my schoolboy fantasy in a real-life occupation that took me all over the world and gave me so much.

In my advancing years, I often ponder the meaning of life and death. I think of those who have gone, of Janie, and of all those fine young men who never came back from the horrors of that bleak Italian mountainside in 1944 or never walked out of that grim sanatorium. But I think, too, of the lovely times I shared, the pleasure of friendships and the thrill of being able to watch so many of the outstanding players who have graced the incomparable game of rugby football.

All manner of things are thrown at us in this world, and we have to accept that our lives will be a pot-pourri of good times and bad. The chief lesson I have learned from it all is that it is people who matter, not baubles or trophies. Those you love, and your closest friends, are more important than anything else, for it is they who help you to cope with whatever hand fate deals you. And it is to the people in my life, my loving family, that I owe everything.

INDEX

INDEX

A SELECTION OF SPORTS TITLES
AVAILABLE FROM TRANSWORLD PUBLISHERS

THE PRICES SHOWN BELOW WERE CORRECT AT THE TIME OF GOING TO PRESS. HOWEVER
TRANSWORLD PUBLISHERS RESERVE THE RIGHT TO SHOW NEW RETAIL PRICES ON COVERS
WHICH MAY DIFFER FROM THOSE PREVIOUSLY ADVERTISED IN THE TEXT OR ELSEWHERE.

81646 2	THE SOUL OF A BUTTERFLY	Muhammad Ali	£6.99
81214 9	MICHAEL SCHUMACHER: DRIVEN TO EXTREMES	James Allen	£8.99
81716 7	THE PLAYER	Boris Becker	£6.99
05376 1	SHIT GROUND NO FANS (H/B)	Jack Bremner	£9.99
81403 6	JENSON BUTTON: MY LIFE ON THE FORMULA ONE ROLLERCOASTER	Jenson Button	£7.99
14003 1	CLOUGH THE AUTOBIOGRAPHY	Brian Clough	£7.99
77076 0	NICE JUMPER	Tom Cox	£6.99
81210 6	A MATTER OF OPINION	Alan Hansen	£6.99
14694 3	VIEW FROM THE SUMMIT	Sir Edmund Hillary	£7.99
81559 8	THE KING	Denis Law	£6.99
81551 2	THE BIG YEAR	Mark Obmascik	£6.99
05474 1	VINCENT O'BRIEN: THE OFFICIAL BIOGRAPHY (H/B)	Jacqueline O'Brien with Ivor Herbert	£25.00
14937 3	BRADMAN'S BEST	Roland Perry	£7.99
50491 6	JENNY PITMAN AUTOBIOGRAPHY	Jenny Pitman	£8.99
14954 3	FOUL PLAY	David Thomas	£7.99
81511 3	DONALD CAMPBELL: THE MAN BEHIND THE MASK	David Tremayne	£7.99

All Transworld titles are available by post from:
Bookpost, PO Box 29, Douglas, Isle of Man, IM99 1BQ
Credit cards accepted. Please telephone +44 (0)1624 677237,
fax +44 (0)1624 670923, Internet http://www.bookpost.co.uk
or e-mail: bookshop@enterprise.net for details.
Free postage and packing in the UK. Overseas customers: allow
£2 per book (paperbacks) and £3 per book (hardbacks).